ALL
IN THE
FAMILY

ALL
IN THE
FAMILY

A Viewer's Companion

David Maska

ALL IN THE FAMILY
A VIEWER'S COMPANION

iUniverse books may be ordered through booksellers or by contacting:

iUniverse
1663 Liberty Drive
Bloomington, IN 47403
www.iuniverse.com
844-349-9409

ISBN: 978-1-6632-6329-2 (sc)
ISBN: 978-1-6632-6330-8 (e)

Library of Congress Control Number: 2024911400

Print information available on the last page.

iUniverse rev. date: 07/26/2024

This book is dedicated to the love of my life Renee. It took me forty-nine years to find you. You were worth the wait. Will you marry me? (we will have to see if there is a second printing to find out if she said yes)

This book is also dedicated in loving memory to Shirley Maska and Rees Padfield.

And to my sister Kim. Thank you for always being there for me.

Contents

Acknowledgements

Sincere thanks to the following people for their love, support, or just plain feigning interest when I would mention this over the last several years:

Ed and Cheyney Bieber and family (Sydney, Jake, Regan, Fifi, Teddy, River, and Toby), Gary Blake, Lizette Cardinas, Jonathan Padfield, Tom and Linda Conran, Melissa Dragovan, Barb MF Eise and her family (David, Connor, Ty, Lexi, and Kelsey), JB Fletcher, Len Grodoski, Jessica Hoffman, Joanne Padfield, Matthew C. Hoffman, Honeybun, Mary Kay Lockhart, Ed Magruder, Max, Leo Mukahirn, Liz Munesue, Elaine Padfield, Mary Ann Nicolella, Ted Okuda, Steve Padfield and family (Nikki, Logan, and Mackenzie (UNO!)), Joe Plochl, Carol Rhunke, Michele and Al Salazar, Bella Stutt, Mark Yurkiw, Christy Zurcher.

Introduction

All in the Family has been a part of my television viewing landscape as far back as I can remember. In the age of home media and streaming, over the years I have watched episodes in no particular order and have always been entertained. It had been some time since I watched the series from beginning to end so I decided to sit down and do just that, and note my thoughts and observations along the way. It was a new show to me in many ways and I was able to look at it with a fresh perspective. What impressed me was how the characters grew and changed from their experiences and if they took an emotional step forward, they rarely took a step back at the expense of a punch line. I was not there for the series premier in 1971; being (almost) one-year old at the time, chances are my parents already put me to bed. Binging the show as an adult, it is not surprising just how well the material holds up. Sure, some of the references are dated but the humanity still shines. It still moved me; it made me laugh and it made me cry. Many times, I found myself doing both at the same time. Fifty-plus years after it first aired, I can still relate to something in each of these characters.

Many people say they've either lived with or known an "Archie Bunker" in their lifetime and could also relate to the other family members of 704 Hauser Street. That was the secret to All in the Family; we all knew people like this. Presented as satire, the series was palatable to a viewing audience who kept the show at the top of the ratings for most of its run.

There are many others out there who can articulate the social impact of the show much better than I. My goal for what follows is not that academic. The origins of this book are meant to be a conversational reference for a show that I have loved all my life. It is a viewer's companion which provides a season-by-season summary. I have included episode highlights, an annotated episode guide including continuity goofs, and an overview of how the characters and show changed along with the country and its viewing habits while the show was on the air. I hope I have accomplished that and hope you enjoy the read.

Family Planning

Sitcoms have been a staple of television ever since its inception. A premise is presented and resolved within a 30-minute timeslot and done so in a humorous way. Classic shows such as I Love Lucy and The Honeymooners provided a template with their stories and characters that continue to influence the genre of the sitcom to this very day. However, sitcoms rarely took chances in dealing with any serious subject matter although when they did, those subjects stayed somewhat safely tucked within the framework of sitcom rules and almost always had a happy ending.

Norman Lear was born on July 7, 1922. His relationship with his father was strained and argumentative. Lear's father would always refer to Norman as a 'meathead' and spout very bigoted and prejudicial points of view. Not surprisingly, his father became the prototype for Archie Bunker. Lear's mother was kind with a big heart and was a huge influence on the character of Edith Bunker. At the end of World War II, Lear headed out West to pursue a career in public relations and publicity. He then teamed with Ed Simmons who was married to Lear's cousin Elaine and the pair embarked on a career to become comedy writers. Within a short period of time, they were writing sketches for Martin and Lewis who were the hottest act in the country in the 1950s.

In the mid-60s, while the country was embroiled in civil unrest and many felt we were fighting an unjust war in Vietnam, the trend in television was that of fantasy and science fiction. Such shows as Get Smart, The Monkees, Batman, and Star Trek broke the mold of traditional television up to that point. Concurrently, shows such as I Dream of Jeannie and Bewitched had their fantasy elements played out within the confines of the traditional sitcom. Still, television in the United States continued to play things relatively safe.

While visiting England in the late 60s, Lear viewed a show called Till Death Us Do Part. In this show the lead character Alf Garnett is a working-class man who has an adoring wife and daughter. Garnett was a very bigoted character and his views were always at odds with his socialist son-in-law. Lear saw much of his father in this character. The interaction between Garnett and his son-in law was reminiscent of arguments Lear used to have with his own father. Lear was inspired to try to adapt this show for a US audience. His partnership with Simmons had dissolved by that time and Lear formed a production company with fellow producer Bud Yorkin. Yorkin began his career in 1954 producing The Tony Martin Show for NBC. The production company was eventually christened

Tandem and although their partnership would dissolve in 1975, the company would go on to produce all the major Lear sitcoms of the 1970's except for The Jeffersons which was produced by Yorkin's T.A.T Production Company. In addition, Tandem produced Diff'rent Strokes, Archie Bunker's Place, Sanford, and Gloria until it ceased operating under that name in 1983.

Relevancy wise, television entertainment in the United States was behind the times. There were signs of life earlier in the decade with solid dramas like Perry Mason, The Twilight Zone, and The Defenders. By the mid-60s, shows like I Spy, That Girl, Julia, and Mod Squad showed promise of what could be done with the medium between casting and subject matter. Even The Brady Bunch, which premiered in 1969 was ground-breaking in its own way by portraying a blended family of two single parents. The Smothers Brothers would increasingly take chances on their weekly CBS variety show with sketches co-written by the likes of Steve Martin, Bob Einstein, and Carl Gottlieb. The show blended social-political commentary and satire including criticism of the Vietnam war, material which was not appreciated by the Lyndon Johnson White House. Pressure over censorship struggles with CBS VP of Network Programming Michael Dann ultimately contributed to the Smothers Brothers dismissal from the network in 1969. They would subsequently sue CBS for breach of contract and win a settlement in 1973. Changes in leadership would follow at CBS within the next few years and while unknown at the time, those events would pave the way to get All in the Family on the air.

THE PILOTS

Lear wrote a pilot script titled **Justice for All** and began to shop it around to the different networks in 1968. The lead character was Archie Justice. Lear originally wanted to cast Mickey Rooney in the lead role however Rooney declined saying that the character was un-American.

Born August 2, 1924, actor Carroll O'Connor honed his skills in the theatre. He sharpened his talents in some off-Broadway productions such as The Big Knife directed by 20-year-old Peter Bogdanovich (his first directorial venture) and Ulysses in Nighttown which co-starred John Astin and was directed by Burgess Meredith. O'Connor also carved a niche for himself on television as a character actor. He had parts in such shows as The Defenders, The Outer Limits, That Girl, and The Time Tunnel. When Sherwood Schwartz was auditioning roles for his upcoming series Gilligan's Island, O'Connor was considered for the role of the Skipper. He did work in feature films as well and Lear was specifically impressed with his performance in the 1966 comedy What Did You Do in the War, Daddy? Lear asked him to read for the part of Archie Justice. O'Connor was familiar with the source material, Til Death

Us Do Part, and recounted a conversation with his wife about the subject matter prior to his audition in a 2000 interview. "I remember saying to my wife Nancy, here's a show – we could never do that here. We could never do this outrageous satire in this country. The American people are not prepared, we're not the kind of people that can swallow this stuff."[1] He picked up on the New York accent from cabbies he had heard over time and scored immediately with Lear. "He was such a touchy character that I wanted to be absolutely sure that if I played it – and I knew how to play him, I knew how to play that guy but I wanted to play it with absolute authenticity."[2] recalled O'Connor. In real life a staunch Democrat, O'Connor had more in common with Mike Stivic than he did with Archie Bunker and he created one of the most iconic characters ever on television.

Jean Stapleton (born January 19, 1923) also came from the Broadway stage. She was involved in several hit musicals such as Bells Are Ringing and Damn Yankees and would reprise her roles in the filmed versions. It was her performance on the stage in Damn Yankees that caught Lear's attention when he asked her to read for the part. Stapleton was not a stranger to O'Connor as she appeared with him on a 1962 episode of the Defenders titled "The Hidden Jungle". Unfortunately, a print of this episode was not available for screening at the time of this writing but according to an interview Stapleton gave to the Archive of American Television, they did share some scenes together. By the time she read for the role of Edith Justice, she already had appeared in dozens of tv shows such as Car 54 Where Are You?, My Three Sons, Dennis the Menace, and Dr. Kildare.

The role of the son-in-law Richard – or Dicke at this stage in development – was of Irish not Polish descent in the pilot and went to actor Tim McIntire. He appeared on television throughout the early 1960s in shows like Wagon Train and Ben Casey. Although he would ultimately be recast, he would continue acting in such shows as the F.B.I, the mini-series Rich Man, Poor Man, and Soap. He also appeared in some feature films, most notably as disc jockey Allan Freed in American Hot Wax (1978) and Brubaker (1980) with Robert Redford. After struggling for years with drug and alcohol addiction, he died at the age of 41 in 1986.

To round out the main players, Lear hired Kelly Jean Peters for the part of Gloria. Up to that point she had appeared on such programs as The Monkees, The Green Hornet, and That Girl. She would continue work in television and is recognizable to M*A*S*H fans as Lt. Louise Anderson in the 1973 episode "Love Story". In support, the part of Lionel is played by D'Urville Martin who also appeared throughout the 60s on television in shows like The Man from U.N.C.L.E. and The Monkees and was instrumental in the blacksploitation film movement. He would be the only actor aside from O'Connor and Stapleton to survive the cut after the first pilot was taped. He went on to appear on television and several films in the 1970s such as Black Caesar and Dolemite. He died in 1984 at the age of 45.

ABC Programming Executive Leonard Goldberg whose network was struggling in third place saw the potential in the script and was the first to take a chance on the series. Goldberg told the E! network in 2000 "I just thought it was so different and it was so shocking that, I thought that was good. I thought we'd get a lot of attention."[3] Lear was given $250,000 to shoot the pilot which commenced on September 29, 1968. There would be some dialog changes in subsequent versions of the pilot both for content and brevity. Archie refers to Lionel as a "smart ass kid" which was changed to "smart aleck kid" by the time the pilot finally aired. An exchange between Archie and Edith about the use of the phrase "Goddamn it" would also be cut. That bit along with several other dialogue cuts would find their way into other episodes of the series once it went to air. Running thirty-five minutes, the pacing of the pilot is much slower and the lines are delivered more deliberately. Archie Justice sports a Dagwood like hairstyle suggesting a representation of a bygone era. Aside from that, he and Edith's characters, while rough around the edges, are pretty well defined. Richard is presented as more of a hippie with a tie-dye shirt and a big peace medallion around his neck which was a direct reflection of 1968 American youth.

Gloria comes across sassy and streetwise lacking the underlying vulnerability that would ultimately round out the character. As the episode unfolds, the kids come across way more argumentative and combative with Archie and the results are uninspired for what the script calls for. The Lionel character is played as more of a wise guy evident in the way he gives a wink to Richard before approaching Archie to discuss things. The studio audience does not seem engaged in the performances. When screened for ABC executives, the room was empty by the time the screening was completed. Goldberg caught up with the President of the network shortly thereafter and was told "We're going to pretend that this never happened."[4] Despite little support from upper management, Goldberg requested a second pilot be shot. With the four principles lacking the chemistry that would ultimately make the show a success, Lear took the opportunity to recast the parts of Richard and Gloria.

On February 16, 1969 the second pilot was taped. Retitled **Those Were the Days**, Chip Oliver replaced Tim McIntire as Richard and while his approach is a little softer, it still is not what the series would need. While he is articulate in his discussions with Archie, this version of Richard comes across more primitive than intelligent - putting Gloria over his shoulder to bring her upstairs as he wants to take advantage of the alone time they have. This was Chip Oliver's sole television credit. He was a linebacker with the Oakland Raiders for two seasons which may account for the direction his character was given. After the 1969 season, he quit the Raiders, joined a commune, and became a vegetarian. Mike Stivic would have been proud of him.

The part of Gloria went to 23-year-old Candice Azzara. She plays Gloria a little closer to the way she would be portrayed in the series. Azzara had only one acting credit prior to taping the pilot and would go on to appear in such shows as Kojak, Barney Miller, and Rhoda as well as feature films Easy Money (alongside Rodney Dangerfield) in 1983, Catch Me if You Can (2002), and In Her Shoes (2005).

While opinions somewhat softened the second time around, ABC ultimately passed on the pilot fearing backlash from affiliates and viewers over the sensitive nature of the material.

Lear's agent shopped the pilot to CBS, the same network who dismissed the Smothers Brothers a year or so earlier in part over controversial material. CBS had been known as the "rural network" throughout the 60s with such hits as Petticoat Junction, Green Acres, The Andy Griffith Show, and the Beverly Hillbillies dominating their schedule. However, by 1970 those sitcoms were showing their age and the network felt they were losing touch with an urban audience. Times were rapidly changing and CBS

President Bob Wood wanted shows on the schedule that more reflected the times and appealed to advertisers and viewers in the larger cities. Unlike the execs at ABC, the pilot impressed programming head Michael Dann yet he shared similar reservations about putting it on the air. He asked Norman Lear to shoot a new pilot and suggested changing the name of the show. Rechristened "All in the Family", Lear agreed and took the opportunity to make two final changes to the main cast as he felt the kids were still not strong enough performers.

24-year-old Rob Reiner (born March 6, 1947) was no stranger to Hollywood. Son of legendary television producer Carl Reiner, he most recently was writing for the Glen Campbell Goodtime Hour. Reiner made his television acting debut in a January 1967 episode of Batman. He went on to appear on The Andy Griffith Show, Gomer Pyle, The Beverly Hillbillies and did audition for the part of Richard for the pilot when it was being touted to ABC. While Lear felt he was too inexperienced at that time, he now felt Reiner was ready for the role. The character was renamed Michael Stivic, who was of Polish descent. Reiner recalled. "When I first read the script, I thought well this is certainly by far the best thing that will ever be on television. The quality, the writing, was so far beyond anything that had been on television up to that point. I just assumed that if it was ever going to get on, it would be on a for a few weeks and then it would go off. It would be as we say - too hip for the room. People artistically would appreciate it but it would just be too rough for people to accept. I figured we'd be on for thirteen weeks and then it would just go off and I would be very proud to have been a part of something that was that special."[5] Reiner continued to make a few appearances on other tv shows during the early run of All in the Family such as The Odd Couple and The Partridge Family.

Sally Struthers (born July 28, 1947) had been a stock performer on The Smothers Brothers Comedy Hour where she caught the attention of Norman Lear. Struthers most recently appeared with Jack Nicholson in the 1970 classic Five Easy Pieces. She was perfect for the role of Gloria. Lear recalled "There was something about that adorable person....so we invited her in and she had everything else to back it up."[6] She was tough when she needed to be but she also had the innocence and sweetness required to provide the balance between Archie and Mike, the two most important men in Gloria's life.

There would be one final casting change with the role of Lionel Jefferson. Mike Evans studied acting at Los Angeles City College and did not have any acting experience prior to being hired for the series. He was perfect for the role and played Lionel as more of an intelligent and sympathetic character; someone who saw through Archie's bigotry and prejudice enough to politely humiliate him yet understood that he really was a good person deep down. Norman Lear commented "the eyes must be laughing at Archie from behind an immobile face."[7] Evans brought a sincerity and believability to the role that was previously lacking and made Lionel more three dimensional and less of a punch line. Their scenes together are some of the most memorable of the early years of the series. Evans would later co-create the hit series Good Times and would continue to portray Lionel Jefferson in the spinoff The Jeffersons for most of its 10-year run.

With the cast finalized, the script was shot for a third time and screened for CBS executives. Michael Dann commented that if they had stronger sitcoms for consideration that season, All in the Family may not have been picked up. With some reservation, he requested 13 episodes. The pilot was passed to CBS VP of Program Practices William Tankersley who was shocked, feeling that the material was "pretty gross"[8] and would have to be softened a bit. Lear and the cast remained optimistic yet skeptical and doubtful that the show would ever air.

Meantime Michael Dann resigned as Head of Programming and was replaced by Fred Silverman who at the time was head of daytime programming and screened the pilot. Silverman shared the vision of CBS President Bob Wood and a show like All in the Family appealed to that vision. Silverman was given the responsibility of finding a timeslot for the show and would eventually order the rural purge of the CBS lineup of bucolic sitcoms at the end of the 1970/71 season.

With CBS on board albeit with some lingering reservation, the question came up as to where to put it on the schedule. The network was still a little nervous and according to Lear, wanted to air the second episode of the series (**Writing the President**) as the premiere almost up to the last minute as they felt it was "far tamer."[9] Lear recalled in a 2010 interview that he told the network "We're gonna jump into the water together and get wet, you can't get wetter than wet. The first script gets us all together wet and that's the one I want to use."[10]. CBS pushed back and Lear, who was concurrently entertaining a feature film deal with United Artists, told the network if the second episode screened first, he was done. Even his family encouraged him to take the film deal as they felt the show would be forced off the air. Having invested so much time and emotion into the project, Lear hung in there and the night before the premiere, CBS acquiesced and scheduled the pilot episode to air first. The network decided to 'hide' the show in their line-up with very little promotion. In the middle of the season on January 12, 1971 it replaced the John Forsythe comedy To Rome with Love on the Tuesday night schedule following The Beverly Hillbillies, Green Acres, and Hee Haw. CBS manned the switchboards with additional operators to handle any backlash from viewers.

Going one step further, the premiere carried a warning prior to airing. Rob Reiner recalled in a 2010 interview "They had a disclaimer which essentially said nothing you are about to see is anything that we want to have anything to do with…as far as we're concerned if you don't watch the next half-hour that would be ok with us."[11] The warning read as follows:

WARNING:

The program you are about to see is ALL IN THE FAMILY. It seeks to throw a humorous spotlight on our frailties, prejudices, and concerns. By making them a source of laughter, we hope to show in a mature fashion just how absurd they really are.

The question remained. Was America ready to "Meet the Bunkers"?

SEASON ONE

The first episode (**Meet the Bunkers**) aired and television audiences were introduced to the residents of 704 Hauser Street in Queens. Using the pilot script, now for a third time, the Bunkers celebrate their 22nd anniversary and Mike and Gloria throw them a surprise brunch. The happy occasion is interrupted of course as Archie and Mike debate everything from race to sex to politics. The switchboards at CBS did not light up at all as feared except for calls from viewers complimenting the episode and liking what they saw. The premier did mediocre ratings wise but over the course of this first shortened season of 13 episodes the show caught on by word of mouth and built a steady audience. The second episode (**Writing the President**) which CBS had pushed to air first at the last minute was standard sitcom fare by comparison.

The show would need to find an audience and as the remaining episodes played out that season, it gained momentum. Those who missed the boat the first time around caught the summer reruns and at the end of the summer repeats, All in the Family was a bona fide hit. However, not everybody was impressed.

1

The success was a marriage between writing and performance. Now that both pilots have surfaced and are available for public viewing one can see just how important casting and chemistry was. "I cast All in the Family but for the miracle of the way those four people worked together, the way their chemistries melded. The fact that in the first place that they were all available at the same time…that multiplicity of relationships was miracle time…that's a gift of the universe."[12] recalled Lear. Once the pace of the dialog was tightened up, the presentation of the material played much better. A 1971 audience appears to be more engaged and ready for this kind of program. It was "recorded on tape before a live audience" so all the laughs and reactions were real which fed and encouraged the performers. In the end the combined talents of Carroll O'Connor, Jean Stapleton, Rob Reiner, and Sally Struthers are what kept people tuning in each week. The characters of Archie, Edith, Mike, and Gloria were people you felt you knew. They were much different than the families on the other sitcoms during its run. You connected with them because everyone knew an "Archie Bunker". In fact, we all knew someone who could identify with each character on the show. Although played out as a satire, the series was very relatable to its audience.

As the show went into production, the relationship between the kids and Archie was more sympathetic. This helped present the tension and disagreements between them because there was love, pathos, and understanding underneath it all. They tried in their own way to learn from one another (many times unknowingly) and over the course of the series each character grew to understand the other a bit more and communicate with more clarity. In comparison to today's age of more agenda driven entertainment, this was a much different approach.

In reviewing the pilot episode, Sue Cameron wrote in the Hollywood Reporter that "All in the Family is either going to be an instant smash or instant disaster....the latter is more likely to occur."[13] While giving perhaps a backhanded compliment that there was finally something relevant on television, she continued "the main problem with this show is that in order to achieve laughs in a family satire, there must first be an underlying feeling of love among all parties. Without that foundation, all that comes out is just plain hate."[14] Such criticism was dismissed by the star of the show. "Critic can say what he wants. Most of them are dumbbells. They don't understand art. They can't create it; they don't know what it is when they see it."[15] opined Carroll O'Connor. In defense of Cameron's comments, the characters are rough around the edges in the earliest of episodes almost as if to define what roles they are going to take on for the remainder of the series. However, as All in the Family continued, the soul of each character evolved in short order. Without that development, each of them would have been nothing more than a one note caricature that provided no depth to what made them tick and relate to each other and the world around them. The show would continue to dabble in shades of gray instead of black and white. Many times, during its nine-year run, an issue was not resolved at the end of an episode. A character's struggles and challenges could be built on and referred to again in a future episode. We were watching a reflection of ourselves played out for comedic and satirical purposes each week which would stimulate discussion amongst the viewing audience.

Carroll O'Connor reflected "I was sure our liberals were going to love us. Archie the right-winger was portrayed as an ignoramus. But I found that liberals want to see only pure villains, unrelieved horror. Liberals were our first and loudest detractors. Conservatives surprised me too; they howled aplenty, but seemed willing to laugh at themselves so long as our jibes were fairly spread around."[16]

Jean Stapleton told TV Guide in 1972 "The show manages to puncture the "intellectual pretense" of Mike, Archie's son-in-law, just as effectively as it does the man-eating bigot."[17]

Archie's heart is in the right place but as O'Connor explained to talk show host Dick Cavett in 1971 "We're presenting the story of a man who is basically a pretty unhappy guy. You people may laugh at him and enjoy him but he's not really making it in the modern world at all. The main thing that makes him happy is this volume of errors that he's grown up with – his racism and bigotry…he's grown up with these beliefs and these misconceptions and they really are now poisoning his life….you must look at Archie as a man who could be getting much more out of his life if he didn't have these burdens on him and these things that have poisoned his life."[18] Archie and Edith both grew up during the depression as discussed in **Archie is Worried About His Job**. Archie knows he will always be a blue-collar working man. He is scared to see the world around him changing while his life stands still, more times than not as the result of his own behavior. He is judge and jury as he passes sentence every week from his beloved living room chair which becomes just as much of a character in the show as the four principles. His defense is to try and "stifle" or "dummy up" something before it gets to him so his life remains unaffected by the changing world around him which keeps moving forward without his input. The theme song says "Those Were the Days" and each week Archie is reminded that the world he once felt secure in is closing in around him and he questions where he fits in. Mike represents a threat to Archie because he is going to college and will be able to get the education Archie was denied because of circumstance, dropping out of high school to support his family when his father lost his job during the depression. While he currently lives off Archie's dime, Mike will ultimately be able to provide more for his 'little girl' in ways Archie never could. However, while Archie feels threatened, he also loves his son-in-law for those exact same reasons. While many of their arguments are rooted in being on opposite sides of an issue, many of their jabs at one another are good old-fashioned ball busting.

In the episode **Judging Books by Covers**, Archie jokes about Mike's friend Roger, played by a pre–General Hospital Tony Geary, being gay only to find out that his longtime friend Steve, a former football player, is a homosexual. The stereotypical epithets are leveled about Roger early in the episode only to see Archie wind up with his foot in his mouth in the closing moments when Steven confirms that not only is Roger not gay but he is.

While being referred to as a "dingbat" by Archie, Edith is really the anchor of their relationship and adores Archie. In **Gloria Discovers Women's Lib** she suggests that she may play and go along with Archie's ranting telling an angry Gloria "How can you be sure that what you see is really how it is?". However, Edith is smart. She knows to give him just enough line then reels him. In some of the initial episodes, her delivery is a little sharper around the edges as she punctuates scenes with dialog that appears more intentional in delivery. Rob Reiner recalled "Archie would just puff himself up and rant and rave and she would, with the most perfect bon mot come under it with the truth and just cut him down to size."[19] As the series matured, the sharpness of her comments dissipated and evolved from the innocence of the character as part of the flow of conversation. Yet they were by no means less lethal as the exasperated Archie would once again be put in his place. As Stapleton commented in a 2000 interview with the Archive of American Television about her character - "a compassionate individual, a peculiar way at arriving at things and thoughts, not very bright, not well educated, and a perception about people that was instinctive – intuitive, and sometimes it was a very sharp understanding. She went right to the root of something. Just a lot of love…unselfish love."[20] The character was patterned after Norman Lear's own mother yet when he spoke with Jean Stapleton about the role, Stapleton wondered how to react to Archie when he was going off on one of his rants. Lear told her "Jean, you're Patty Andrews. You're the middle sister in the Andrews Sisters and what's going through your head is don't sit under the apple tree with anyone else but me and for some reason she loved that, glommed onto that, and never lost that. Her mind was in a happy place, someplace else, tuned him out."[21] There are qualities of Stan Laurel or Gracie Allen in Edith's presence which is filled with kindness and generosity juxtaposed with Archie's every man for himself attitude.

The episode **Edith Has Jury Duty** gives Edith center stage. She is picked for jury duty for a young Hispanic man accused of murder. She considers this to be an honor and highlight of her life which otherwise is spent in servitude to her husband. Inspired by the classic play Twelve Angry Men, she is the lone holdout in a murder trial. Edith feels the pressure from another juror who has similar views like Archie to change her verdict so everyone can go home. You really get to understand the innocence of her character. Edith sees things for what they are. She does not question them nor is she suspicious. She truly loves unselfishly and sees the world through an honesty rarely seen in television characters. She sticks to her guns and as it turns out, the young man was innocent.

Mike's father died when he was young so warts and all, Archie is the father he never had and Mike the son Archie never had. They need each other even though they have two completely different views of the country much the same as Norman Lear had with his father. Archie has lived a life that Mike only reads about in his schoolbooks and as the series goes on Mike is reminded that he as well is not always right about everything. In the classic episode **Success Story** Archie's friend Eddie Frazer (played by William Windom) pays him a visit. Eddie is very successful and what Archie does not know is that he is estranged from his son whom Eddie offers $500 to for 5 minutes of his time. He is only using visiting Archie as an excuse to kill time. Mike overhears the conversation Eddie has with his son knowing how much Eddie means to him, would not dare burst Archie's bubble. Archie may not have the wealth and success that his friend has but he does have the love of his son-in-law and is able to communicate with him.

In an episode **Now That You Know the Way, Let's be Strangers** co-written by Rob Reiner, Mike's hippie friends come to stay the night. Archie is not comfortable having an unmarried couple stay under his roof. As the couple becomes increasingly inflexible about the arrangement, Mike stands up for Archie and asks them to look at some alternatives. While Mike has more in common with the hippies than Archie, he is evolving past the stubbornness that ultimately collapsed the hippie movement in the early 70's. When push comes to shove, Mike does understand the value of the compromise and ultimately sides with Archie.

Although Gloria is now married, the bond between her and her father is still very strong. In the episode **Gloria is Pregnant** both Mike and Archie are upset at first to hear this news. They are both concerned that Mike is not in a position yet to provide for a child. After a heated exchange about the benefits of link vs. patty sausage over the breakfast table, an exasperated Archie leaves the house to go out for his meal. He has some time to absorb the news and changes his position. When he comes home later with a giant panda bear for the baby, he is unaware that while he was gone Gloria miscarried. He goes up to her room for a visit and sits next to the bed gently holding her hand. There is not much in the way of dialog exchanged between the two actors. The conversation happens through expression and close-up. Archie cannot find the words but his presence is all Gloria needs at that moment. It is scenes such as these that gave Archie Bunker depth and kept him from being a caricature. The acting is understated and honest. You can really feel the love between father and daughter in this moment.

For the most part, the Bunkers are isolated from the world around them in the earliest of the series episodes. There may be a visitor or two but they are mostly used as devices to highlight the issue that is being discussed that week. Over the course of the first season and as the series blossomed, the outside world would interact more with the Bunkers and we as the viewer would see situations play out in front of us instead of just being discussed via third person.

"Civil rights issue (sic) went right through the series with our black neighbors"[22] Jean Stapleton said to the Archive of American Television in 2000. "That was marvelous stuff - uncovering bigotry and uncovering it with humor. There's nothing like humor to burst what seems to be an enormous problem. Humor reduces it to nothing and wipes it out."[23] The Jeffersons have moved in next door and after unsuccessfully petitioning to have them leave the neighborhood in **Lionel Moves Into the Neighborhood**, Archie unknowingly accepts a dinner invitation in the season finale **The First and Last Supper**. Of course, Archie has tickets to the Mets game and forces Edith to lie about spraining her ankle to get out of the dinner. The Jeffersons offer to bring the food over so they will not have to cancel. Archie meets Lionel's father George who proceeds to hysterically argue with Archie that God is black. As the Jeffersons prepare to leave it turns out they were lying too. It is George's brother Henry who has been sent over in his place so George can go to Shea Stadium to watch the Mets! We will not meet George Jefferson until the season four-episode **Henry's Farewell** but in the meantime, Henry will keep Archie plenty busy. Henry was played by Mel Stewart who, along with fellow castmate Rob Reiner, previously was a member of the improv troupe The Committee.

Lear found that he had two big fans of the show in Bob Finkel who oversaw the Emmy Awards program for the 1970/71 season and Johnny Carson who would be hosting the ceremony. According to Lear, he received a call from Finkel saying he would like to feature the Bunkers in the opening of the Emmy telecast to introduce them to a mass audience. A short introduction scene was written with the Bunkers preparing to watch the show.

Prolific television director John Rich would helm all 13 of the first season episodes and had experience with ensemble shows, directing over 40 episodes of the Dick Van Dyke Show, for which he won an Emmy. Jean Stapleton recalled "it was free theatre and I was very comfortable in that. That laughter just feeds you as an actor. And if something was non-character, we were allowed to discuss it and then go back and fix it. Our director John Rich (and Paul Bogart) said you are in a free theatre - enjoy it."[24] In a 1976 appearance on Dick Clark's American Bandstand, O'Connor told the audience that they were allowed to improvise during rehearsal but once the show went in front of the cameras, improvising was not allowed so as not to ruin the take and rhythm of a scene. John Rich's credits also included episodes of Gilligan's Island, The Brady Bunch, The Jeffersons, Maude, Good Times, and Barney Miller. Rich would direct most of the episodes of the series for its first four seasons and was given the added responsibilities of producer at the start of season three. This helped tremendously with continuity and pacing. There is both a theatrical and cinematic style to his direction and scenes are punctuated with close ups to enhance a dramatic or comedic moment. This would become a hallmark of the series and leave an impression on production long after his departure.

All in the Family was the first major writing gig for Don Nicholl who would go on to pen over thirty episodes over the first five seasons of the show in addition to serving as script consultant, script supervisor, and story editor for over 75 episodes in the first five seasons. He would also become the executive producer in season five.

A soundtrack album was released to stores in 1971 which featured bits from the series' first 13 episodes. When the Emmy Awards for the 1970/71 season were handed out, all in the Family brought home three statuettes for Jean Stapleton (Outstanding Continued Performance by an Actress in a Leading Role in a Comedy Series) and to Norman Lear (for Outstanding New Series and Outstanding Series).

season one episodes

Meet the Bunkers 1-12-71
Mike and Gloria throw a surprise wedding anniversary brunch for Archie and Edith and discuss everything from sex to race relations.

Episode notes:
- In the original pilot, the flowers Lionel buys cost 50 cents. In this episode they are a dollar. The cost of flowers must have gone up since 1968.
- Mike Evans makes his first appearance as Lionel Jefferson in this episode.

Writing the President 1-19-71

Mike and Archie decide to write separate letters to Richard Nixon.

Episode notes:
- The dialogue about Archie having a black friend named Roundtree Cumberbatch was originally in the pilot script but cut out.
- This is one of a handful of episodes this season which has incidental music between some scenes and over the closing episode credit titles.

Archie's Aching Back 1-26-71

Sniffing out a potential payday, Archie fakes a back injury to collect after an accident while driving Munson's cab.

Episode notes:
- This is the first mention of Archie moonlighting as a cab driver to earn some extra money.
- The Bunkers family doctor here is named Dr. Ferguson yet later in the series it will change to Dr. Shapiro.
- This episode marks the first mention and appearance of Archie's legal counsel Rabinowitz, Rabinowitz, and Rabinowitz.
- Mike Evans makes another appearance as Lionel Jefferson.
- Another snippet of dialog from the first pilot pops up here when Archie mentions to Lionel about

his father working as a janitor at the Hemstead apartments.

- This is the first reference of Lionel's father buying a cleaning store.
- This is one of three episodes written by Stanley Ralph Ross who penned many episodes of Batman in the 1960s as well as episodes of The Man from U.N.C.L.E and The Monkees. Ross would go on to develop the series Wonder Woman for television.
- Character actor George Furth (Whitney Fitzroy IV) makes his first of two appearances on the series.
- Richard Stahl makes his first of three appearances in the series here playing the role of attorney Clarence V. Marshall. Stahl had over 100 acting credits including appearances on That Girl, The Partridge Family, and Murder, She Wrote.

Archie Gives Blood 2-2-71

Archie is concerned about where the blood he donates will go.

Episode notes:

- This is the first episode where Archie mentions serving in Folger Italy during World War II. This part of Archie's identity comes from Norman Lear himself who served in the Air Force during World War II.
- This episode features incidental music.

- Mike Evans makes another appearance as Lionel Jefferson.
- This is the first of three All in the Family appearances for Jeannie Linero (billed here as Jeanie Linero). She made several appearances on episodic TV in the 1970s and may be best known as Sonny Corleone's mistress Lucy Mancini in the Godfather.

Judging Books by Covers 2-9-71
Archie thinks Mikes friend Roger is gay only to discover that a longtime friend of his is a homosexual.

Episode notes:
- This episode marks the first mention and appearance of Kelcy's Bar.
- Bob Hastings plays the role of Kelcy. A veteran character actor, he was the voice of Archie Andrews on radio and the raven in the clock on The Munsters. Amid hundreds of guest starring roles on TV he is probably best known as Lt. Elroy Carpenter on McHale's Navy (1962-1966)
- Barney is played by Billy Halop who appeared in both the stage and screen versions of Dead End. Halop would eventually be recast as Munson while Allan Melvin would assume the role of Barney on the series.
- Anthony Geary who plays Roger would go on to greater fame as Luke Spencer in the soap opera General Hospital.

Gloria is Pregnant 2-16-71

Gloria announces she is pregnant but after some complications she loses the baby.

Episode notes:
- The exchange about link vs. patty sausage is another bit of dialog which was excised from the original pilot script.
- This is yet another episode that features incidental music between scenes.
- Mike Evans appears again as Lionel Jefferson.
- This is the final episode of the first season to feature a reprise of "Those Were the Days" in the closing credits before continuing with the closing theme "Remembering You".

Now That You Know the Way,
Let's Be Strangers 2-23-71

Mike's hippie friends want to stay the night but Archie is uncomfortable since they are not married.

Episode notes:
- Mike's friend Paul Goodrow is said to have been his best man at his wedding yet in the season three-episode **Mike and Gloria's Wedding** he is nowhere to be found.
- This is the first series writing credit for Don Nicholl.

- If you look closely during the tag, you can see the overhead microphone in frame when they are trying to wake Archie.
- This is the final episode to have incidental music.
- Paul's friend Jeff Walker is played by Corey Fischer who also appeared on M*A*S*H and Welcome Back, Kotter. The actor will make another appearance in season two.

Lionel Moves Into the Neighborhood 3-2-71

Lionel announces that his family has bought a house in Archie's neighborhood.

Episode notes:

- This is the first episode to feature Isabel Sanford as Louise Jefferson.
- Mike Evans makes another appearance as Lionel Jefferson.
- Lionel mentions that along with him – his mother, father, and aunt are moving in. We will never meet the aunt and there is no mention of his Uncle Henry who will be featured in several episodes over the next three seasons.
- In their first exchange, Archie and Mrs. Jefferson ask each other what happened on Julia and The Doris Day Show respectively the night before.
- Vincent Gardinia plays Jim Bowman, the man who sells his house to the Jeffersons. He would return

to the series in season three and eventually be cast as Frank Lorenzo in season four.
- Archie makes mention that the McNab's used to live in the neighborhood however they are referenced in subsequent episodes so they are indeed still residents of Hauser Street.

Edith Has Jury Duty 3-9-71
Edith is the lone holdout on a jury for a murder trial.

Episode notes:
- The story for this episode was written by Susan Harris who would go on to create the classic sitcoms Soap and The Golden Girls.
- This is the first of two appearances of Holly Irving as the Bunker's neighbor Clara Weidermeyer.

Archie Is Worried About His Job 3-16-71
Worried he will be laid off from work, Archie cannot sleep.

Episode notes:
- This is the first mention of Archie's co-workers Black Elmo, Little Emmanuel, and Stretch Cunningham.
- This is the second and final appearance of Holly Irving as Clara Weidermeyer.
- In what is an otherwise chaotic episode, there is a quiet exchange between Archie and Edith where he discusses the impact the depression had on his father.

- The night watchman (Harry Feeney) is played by veteran character actor Burt Mustin whose career dates to the earliest days of television. He would return to All in the Family later in the series as Mr. Quigley.
- Sandy Kenyon appears as Dave the cop and makes his first of three appearances on the show. Kenyon had dozens of tv credits to his name from Hogan's Heroes to Andy Griffith and M*A*S*H but perhaps most notably to classic TV fans as Magellan in the season two episode of the Twilight Zone "The Odyssey of Flight 33". He will return in the season six-episode **Archie the Hero** and **Bogus Bills** from the show's final season.
- Jack Perkins (the drunk) also appeared in many tv shows from Get Smart to the Lucy Show and Happy Days.

Gloria Discovers Women's Lib 3-23-71
Gloria struggles with her identity and wants to be treated by Michael as an equal partner

Episode notes
- Mike Evans makes another appearance as Lionel Jefferson.

Success Story 3-30-71

Archie's friend Eddie Frazier pays him a visit if only to kill time while he tries to reconnect with his estranged son who wants nothing to do with him.

Episode notes:

- Eddie Frazier is played by William Windom who starred in the early/mid-60s sitcom the Farmer's Daughter and acted in over 250 episodes of episodic television including a recurring role as Dr. Seth Hazlitt on Murder, She Wrote.
- Len Lesser (Billy Pendergast) was no stranger to television appearing on dozens of sitcoms and may be best known to modern audiences as Uncle Leo on the classic 90s sitcom Seinfeld.
- George Savalas (Joe Frouge) is the brother of Telly Savalas and co-starred with him on Kojak as Detective Stavros.

The First and Last Supper 4-6-71

In the season one finale, Archie tries to weasel his way out of a dinner invitation to the Jeffersons home.

Episode notes:

- This is Mel Stewart's first appearance Henry Jefferson although he is listed as George Jefferson in the closing credits.
- Mike Evans returns as Lionel Jefferson.

- Isabel Sanford appears as Louise Jefferson in this episode.
- Henry is introduced at the end of the episode as Louise's brother-in-law.
- William (Billy) Benedict, perhaps best known for his appearances in the East Side Kids / Bowery Boys film series' makes his first of two appearances as Archie's neighbor Jimmy McNab.

SEASON TWO

When All in the Family returned for its sophomore season in September 1971 it was the most popular show in the country. Word of mouth propelled the Bunkers to the zeitgeist of culture during the summer reruns and the other networks started to take notice. Norman Lear would develop another show, while not taking screen credit, based on a UK property Steptoe and Son. The show, titled Sanford and Son was NBCs answer to All in the Family. Featuring Redd Foxx as foul-mouthed and bigoted junk dealer Fred G. Sanford, the show finished at number six for the season and would go on to run for 6 years on the Peacock network.

All in the Family no longer required a warning for viewers as it did in the early episodes. It was pulled from the Wednesday night timeslot and placed as the lead-in for CBS's Saturday night lineup. All in the Family was a hit and true to his word, Fred Silverman made sure there was not a single ear of corn to be found on the 1971-72 CBS schedule.

The writing team of Michael Ross and Bernie West joined the staff in season two. Prior to joining the staff of All in the

Family, they were stand-up comedians and this was their first major assignment. They would serve as story editors, script supervisors, and script editors through season five and would take on production duties in that season as well. Along with Don Nicholl, they really gave the show the bite and edge which made it successful and memorable.

As season two unfolds the outside world not only influences the Bunker's discussions that we are witness to week after week, the characters become even more of an integral part of the story lines. This gives Archie so much more to play off of as his convoluted logic continues to clash with the ever-changing world around him.

In **Edith Writes a Song**, there is $30 in the Bunker family pot. Edith, Mike, and Gloria want to use the money to publish a song for a poem Edith has written. In response to a rash of robberies in the area, Archie wants to use the money to buy a recorded attack dog home defense system and gun to defend his house. Later in the episode when the Bunkers have a break in, the robbers, hilariously played by Cleavon Little and Demond Wilson, turn the tables on Archie when the gun he has purchased to defend his house is now in their hands. The robbers not only make fun of Archie for his bigoted comments but they also make fun of Mike who thinks he understands their struggles because of what he has studied in his sociology class. Whereas Mike is usually correcting everyone, this is the first time someone he thinks he understands has put him in his place. The robbers continue to banter back and forth about life in the ghetto and it is Edith through her innocence and kindness who ultimately puts things in perspective stating "I don't know how you can laugh through all that misery." "Practice lady…practice" is all they can say. In the end, in exchange for Edith singing her song the robbers decide to give the Bunkers their belongings back including the gun once the clip has been removed. A stunned Archie sits paralyzed while the robbers leave through the front door. The show took some criticism that it was perhaps 'too liberal' in the way it handled this event. The counter point suggests that good people do sometimes resort to desperate measures to survive.

In the episode **Flashback: Mike Meets Archie** co-written by Rob Reiner, we are celebrating the Stivic's one year anniversary. It is the first of many times in the series where we take a trip down memory lane and recount the early days of Mike and Gloria's relationship. In the flashback sequences Mike looks more like the Richard character from the first pilot in 1968 and immediately clashes with Archie over the events of the day. Mike loves his country just as much as Archie yet feels he has the right to protest when he feels there has been an injustice. Archie takes the side of standing by his country right or wrong. This point of view will come back to bite Archie later in the season in the episode **Archie and the FBI**. There is no other scene in these earliest of series episodes that shows how much fear Archie has of losing his daughter to another man. When Gloria wants to talk about Michael, Archie tries to change the subject. He deflects talking about how they are going to watch the fights together on Friday night and starts to play box with Gloria. She presses on and stops him saying "Daddy I'm too old for this now I'm not your little girl anymore." "Don't you never tell me that" a crushed Archie says. "She actually didn't know that (Archie) did or said anything wrong until she married Michael and he opened her eyes. Archie's soft spot in his heart is for his daughter and Gloria's soft spot in her heart, until her child came along, was her dad. She knew that he said things that weren't right but she's crazy about him."[25] Struthers recalled.

All in the Family reflected the times and, in **The Blockbuster**, it deals with a problem that was a reality within the real estate industry in the 1970s. Agents would put fear in white neighborhoods by making them think minorities would move in and destroy property values. Once they would buy the house, they would in turn sell it to minorities at inflated prices. Mike explains to Archie that what he is participating in is illegal. All Archie sees are dollar signs and the opportunity to move out to California to work with his cousin who has made a success of himself. While Edith does not agree with Archie, she says she will go along with whatever he wants. Once Archie finds out that his cousin is in bad shape financially – perhaps worse shape than he is himself, he changes his tune and decides not to sell. He has absorbed all that has been said to him by his family yet he claims their thoughts as his own. While his greed no doubt motivates his decision, he goes to warn the neighbors of this man at the end of the episode.

Archie finds out that **The Insurance is Cancelled** on the same day he learns that he must let one of his workers go; Little Emanuel (a Puerto Rican), Black Elmo, or Stretch Cunningham. While Archie cannot understand why the insurance is cancelled, it is explained to him that with minorities moving in around his neighborhood he is now in a high-risk area. Archie argues this but is told that it is just how the system operates. Although he knows in his heart he is doing the wrong thing, Archie winds up firing Emanuel who then shows up at the house wanting to know why. While Emanuel is clearly his best worker and Stretch Cunningham is nothing but a goof, Archie tries to apply the same logic to Emanuel as the insurance agent applied to him. Archie explains that it's just the system. When asked by Emanuel where he can go to talk to "this system", Archie does not have an answer. He is lost because he himself does not understand how a system he has believed in has discarded him. Archie is a victim of the same discrimination that he has applied to Emanuel. At episodes end, all Archie has succeeded in doing is making his work life tougher as his bigotry and prejudice have held him back from doing the right thing.

Bea Arthur comes to assist Edith in taking care of the ailing household who has come down with the flu in **Cousin Maude's Visit**. Archie finds a formidable opponent in Maude who puts Archie in his place. Bea Arthur was veteran of the stage when Norman Lear chose her for the part of Maude. She was a Tony Award winner for Mame in 1966. Her appearance in this episode was so strong and well received, Lear began developing a show around the character. For the last episode of the season, a backdoor pilot[1]* was taped and the following season, Maude, flawed in as many was as Archie but from the liberal perspective, premiered in her own series. She is best known today as the caustic Dorothy Zbornak on the hit series The Golden Girls (1985-1992)

---

[1] a backdoor pilot is a way to financially shoot a pilot for a new series utilizing the budget of an existing series then embedding the pilot somewhere during the run of the existing series.

Christmas Day at the Bunkers is the first of several classic Holiday episodes for the series albeit not always involving happy themes. Archie makes a mistake at work which excludes him from his Christmas bonus. He is too proud to share the news with his family. Edith has figured it out but does not let on so as not to embarrass Archie. When the kids tease him about the gifts they have received, Edith speaks up for her defenseless husband. Henry Jefferson stops by dressed as Santa Claus and like their Jesus argument, debates with Archie that Santa is black. Although they may not have exchanged a lot in material things, in the end Archie realizes that it is not such a bad Christmas after all as he is loved and with his family.

Archie has found a new insurance company and must leave dinner to go drop the payment off in **The Elevator Story**. It is a first for the series in that all the action takes place outside of the Bunker's home. Once in the elevator, Archie is surrounded by a successful black businessman played by the great Roscoe Lee Brown, a Puerto Rican man (played by Hector Elizondo) and his pregnant wife, and a neurotic woman played by Eileen Brennan. Archie's worst fears are realized when the elevator comes to a stop and he is trapped with everyone. Carroll O'Connor became more vocal in the creative process and yield more power on the set which would many times cause ill feeling between he and creator Norman Lear. In this episode, the script called for a more comedic ending and O'Connor had a disagreement with Lear in how the end of the episode should be played out when the pregnant woman gives birth in the elevator. "Carroll O'Connor never met a first draft he liked"[26] recalled Norman Lear. O'Connor reflected "The stage was set for plenty of satirical fun. But we were burdened with a "situation"; it was thought to be a real howl....The birth was tightly woven into the script and I was sure the way it was written, crudely and incredibly, would evoke audience revulsion and not only destroy a basically funny episode, but risk deep public disappointment in the series." "I first expressed myself very coolly, as was my habit. Then, encountering a hint of disagreement, I did something else that was my habit: I yelled bloody murder!...I launched my script toward the ceiling and strolled off the set."[27] "(I was) asserting my right to have a veto over the writing and a creative part in the writing. (Norman) did not want to share that authority with me so it became the terrible struggle taking it away from him and hurting his feelings and he hurting mine."[28] he would defend. A meeting was called with O'Connor, Lear, and episode director John Rich where a compromise was reached. "We found a way to save the childbirth and make it a touching sequence. But we saved the satire and the fun too, and the completed episode was very satisfying."[29] When O'Connor returned to tape the episode, he turned in a very poignant performance. As you hear the baby being born, the camera focuses on Archie and we are experiencing the event with him through his eyes. His anger and frustration gradually melt into happiness. It shows that no matter how bigoted Archie may be there is still a part of him inside where race, creed, or color do not exist and his prejudice surrenders to the miracle of new life. Rob Reiner summarized in 2000 "Those arguments for uncomfortable as they were at times between Norman and Carroll actually wound up making a better product."[30]

An investigation by a government agent puts Archie on the defensive in **Archie and the FBI**. The Government is going around performing background checks on Archie and some of his co-workers. While the rest of the family tries to keep Archie calm, the paranoia of his generation who grew up during the Communist witch hunts in the early 1950s gets the best of Archie and his best buddy Larry Grundy. The initial nervousness of the situation soon gives way to a full fight between these two longtime friends (reminiscent of the classic 1960 episode of the Twilight Zone "The Monsters Are Due on Maple Street"). After many harsh words are exchanged, Archie receives a call saying that the investigation was a mistake. Edith says they can go back to being best buddies but the damage has been done. Larry leaves the house without saying a word and his departure is punctuated by the sound of the door closing on their long friendship which startles Archie. The camera tightens in on Archie so his thoughts are isolated with us. Archie says "All that best buddy stuff, it's all for kids anyhow" knowing well that he has lost a valuable friendship to his own paranoia and prejudice.

"Jean Stapleton is a brilliant, brilliant comedienne" recalled Rob Reiner in a 2004 interview. "It's one thing to create a great character and have some great writing but you have to have somebody that will deliver and she delivered big time."[31] Stapleton takes center stage in **Edith's Problem**. Edith is dealing with mood swings and she takes it out quite uncharacteristically on the rest of the family with hilarious results. Gloria suggests that she might be going through menopause. It is another topic that television did not explore in the early 70s. You feel so sorry for Edith as she is concerned that Archie will not love her anymore. The topic is not merely used as a backdrop for jokes and one liners. It deals with the event in a compassionate way and the humor is derived from how the characters we have come to know react to what is going on in their lives. Edith and Mike share a scene together where she confesses her fears and Mike consoles her. Like the scene with Archie and Gloria in the season one episode **Gloria is Pregnant**, Mike provides Edith with some needed emotional comfort and reassurance. Archie does his best to be sweet to her until he cannot take it anymore and blows up. When Edith reacts sweetly and says she now knows Archie loves her, it quickly changes back to anger and another trip to the "groinocologist" for Archie and Edith.

Carroll O' Connor once said of Archie Bunker that "I think he looked in the mirror and saw a fine man every time except when he hurt Edith's feelings then he looked in the mirror and saw a rat and then he was anxious to make it up to her. But other times no, he saw a fine man – a fine upstanding, intelligent man who knew the answer to things."[32] In **Archie and Edith Alone**, the episode is bookended by appearances from Mike and Gloria and is the first episode of the series to really examine the relationship between Archie and Edith after he hurts her during an argument. Edith wants to dance but Archie would prefer that she stay quiet so he can read his paper. He agrees to play cards but a fight ensues after Edith allows him to win. In a heated exchange he tells Edith that she (ain't) human and really hurts her. It is a daring move to push a lead character of a show that far with an audience as you really feel angry at Archie but you stay with him because you know he feels terrible for what he said. Edith demands an apology and Archie tries to repair the damage he has caused. He fumbles to find the words she wants to hear but an apology is hard for him to articulate. Edith bails him out by saying the words for him then gives him credit for saying sorry. They embrace and kiss and it wins the audience back. At that very moment, the kids return home where Mike says "Oh geeze, they're at it again." There will be more relationship challenges for Archie and Edith and future episodes will further explore the depth of their love for one another.

One of the shows biggest supporters was Sammy Davis Jr. and he desperately wanted to make an appearance although the show was not known for having guest stars. In **Sammy's Visit**, while moonlighting for Munson's Cab Company Archie has Sammy in the cab as a fare. Sammy leaves his briefcase behind and comes to 704 Houser Street to get it on his way to the airport. Archie tries his best to keep his visit under wraps but within time every neighbor appears to crawl out of the woodwork to stop in and say hi. The kids apologize for Archie's behavior. Lionel acknowledges that Archie is not a bad guy despite the things he says. Before the visit wraps up, Sammy has just one request of Archie that they take a picture together. Right as the picture is snapped, Sammy plants a big kiss on Archie's cheek. The look on Archie's face is priceless and the audience has one of the most sustained laughs in the series history.

"We were kidding American attitudes and the artistic term for that is satire. We were having fun with these attitudes. We weren't promoting anything but…Norman and I and the cast knew what we were up to."[33] Carroll O'Connor recalled. As season two wrapped, the series was on a hot streak with the perfect blend of drama and comedy.

All in the Family had a strong showing at the Emmy Awards that year with 11 nominations and 7 wins, Carroll O'Conner, Jean Stapleton, and Sally Struthers each took home Outstanding Performance statuettes. John Rich won for directing **Sammy's Visit**. Burt Styler won for writing **Edith's Problem**, and Norman Dewes received an award for Outstanding Achievement in Live or Tape Sound Mixing for **The Elevator Story**. All in the Family again won the Emmy for Outstanding Series. It also won at the Golden Globes for Best TV Show and Best TV Actor for Carroll O'Connor with the remaining three cast members all nominated.

season two episodes

The Saga of Cousin Oscar 9-18-71
Archie's Cousin Oscar dies in his attic leaving Archie to foot the bill for services.

Episode notes
- Archie makes mention in this episode of having a sister Alma and brother Phil. When his brother is next mentioned in the season three-episode **Lionel Steps Out** his name will be Fred and no further mention will be made of him having a sister.
- Edith says she has two sisters Gertrude and Helen.
- Dr. Kelly again is known as the Bunker's physician.
- This is the second and final appearance of William (Billy) Benedict as Jim McNab.

- While referred to multiple times in the series, the character of Reverend Felcher makes his only appearance in this episode.
- Character actor M. Emmet Walsh appears in this episode.
- Peggy Rea makes her first of two appearances as Cousin Bertha.
- Isabel Sanford returns as Louise Jefferson.
- Jack Grimes makes his first of two appearances as the undertaker Mr. Grimes. He will return in the season four-episode **Archie and the Computer**.
- while originally spoken by a staff announcer over the closing credits in season one, beginning with this episode through the end of season eight, Rob Reiner says "All in the Family was recorded on tape in front of a live audience."

Gloria Poses in the Nude 9-25-71

Mike becomes increasingly jealous after he initially agrees to Gloria posing in the nude for his old friend Szabo.

Episode notes
- There is a new opening credit sequence at the piano beginning with this episode.
- This is the first episode that mentions Mike is from Chicago.
- Mike Evans makes another appearance as Lionel Jefferson.

- David Soul plays Szabo Daborba. He would gain fame later in the decade by portraying officer Ken Hutchinson in the iconic series Starsky and Hutch.
- This episode marks the first writing collaboration for Michael Ross and Bernie West.

Archie in the Lock-Up 10-2-71

Archie winds up in jail going to rescue Mike from a protest.

Episode notes

- Sgt. Pulaski is played by veteran TV actor Allan Melvin who appeared on everything from The Phil Silvers Show to The Brady Bunch (as Sam the Butcher). He also voiced classic characters for Hanna-Barbera shows such has Drooper on the Banana Splits and Magilla Gorilla. He would be cast as Archie's friend Barney Heffner starting with **Sammy's Visit** later in season two. Melvin would become more of a featured player later in the series and when the show transitioned to Archie Bunker's Place in 1979.
- Mike Evans makes another appearance as Lionel Jefferson.
- Ken Lynch makes his first of two appearances on the show as the guard Callahan.
- Corey Fischer makes his second and final appearance in the series as the Jesus freak Archie meets in jail.

- If you look closely this is the first time you see the American flag pin on Archie's jacket lapel which would be a staple of his wardrobe for the remainder of the series.

Edith Writes a Song 10-9-71
Two burglars break into the Bunker house and hold them hostage after robbing a jewelry store.

Episode notes
- Cleavon Little may be best known as Sherriff Bart in the 1974 Mel Brooks classic Blazing Saddles.
- Demond Wilson played Lamont Sanford for six seasons on Sanford and Son. He would go on to star in the one season sitcoms Baby...I'm Back! and The New Odd Couple with co-star Ron Glass. He became a minister in 1984.
- Mike Evans makes another appearance as Lionel Jefferson.

Flashback: Mike Meets Archie 10-16-71
While celebrating Mike and Gloria's first wedding anniversary, they recall the first time Mike came over to meet Archie.

The Election Story 10-30-71
Archie gets wound up about who everyone else is voting for in the local election only to find out he is not registered.

Episode notes
- This episode marks the first mention of Ferguson's Market.
- Mike Evans makes a return appearance as Lionel Jefferson.
- Isabel Sanford returns as Louise Jefferson.
- Barbara Cason stars as Claire Packer. She will return to the series as a nurse in the season six-episode **Birth of the Baby part II** and as Miss Critchen in the final season episode **Edith Gets Fired**.

Edith's Accident 11-5-71
Edith leaves a note on a parked car after a runaway shopping cart dents it with a can of cling peaches (in heavy syrup)

- Barnard Hughes makes his first of three appearances as Father John Majeski

The Blockbuster 11-13-71
Archie considers selling the house after a shady real estate agent offers him more than its value.

Episode notes
- We learn that 20 years ago, Archie paid $14,000 for his home and he is being offered $35,000
- this is the second and final appearance of Peggy Rea as cousin Bertha. She will return as Edith's

friend Martha Birkhorn in the season nine-episode **Barney, the Gold Digger**. She can also be spotted (unbilled) as a wedding guest later this season in part II of **Flashback: Mike and Gloria's Wedding**.

- Mike Evans returns as Lionel Jefferson.
- While Archie embraces the thought of moving to California in this episode, he will denounce it in the final episodes of season eight when Mike accepts a job on the West Coast

Mike's Problem 11-20-71

Mike has performance anxiety while he studies for his exams.

Episode notes

- While the character does not make an appearance, this is the first episode that mentions Sybil Goolie.
- Gloria consults Dr. Kermit on this issue instead of the family doctor Dr. Kelly.
- Mel Stewart makes a return appearance as Henry Jefferson.
- Tommy, identified in the credits as "the Bartender" at Kelcy's is played this time by Brendan Dillon.
- Archie mentions running into childhood friend Bummie Fencel on the subway and that he has not seen him in thirty-seven years. Bummie will pay a visit to the Bunkers later in the season seven-episode **Archie's Secret Passion**.

The Insurance is Canceled 11-27-71

Archie finds out his homeowner's insurance has been cancelled.

Episode notes

- Rafael Campos co-stars as Little Emanuel. He appeared in many other TV shows such as The Streets of San Francisco and Rhoda.

The Man in the Street 12-4-71

Archie is interviewed for a man in the street segment but the family TV goes out and they scramble to find a working set.

Episode notes

- Mike Evans returns as Lionel Jefferson.

Cousin Maude's Visit 12-11-71

With only Edith to take care of an ailing Archie, Mike, and Gloria, cousin Maude comes to help.

Christmas Day at the Bunkers 12-18-71

The Bunkers to their best to celebrate the Holiday even though Archie did not receive a Christmas bonus.

Episode notes

- Noam Pitlik plays Wilbur. Pitlik appeared in several sitcoms in the 1960s including Hogan's Heroes and Get Smart. He would also find success behind the camera directing most of the episodes of Barney Miller.

- Mike Evans makes another appearance as Lionel Jefferson.
- Mel Stewart returns as Henry Jefferson.
- Isabel Sanford makes a return appearance as Louise Jefferson.

The Elevator Story 1-1-72

Archie winds up trapped in an elevator while trying to drop off an insurance payment.

Episode notes

- The family is celebrating Edith's birthday in this episode.
- Roscoe Lee Brown makes the first of two appearances in this episode. In a career that spanned almost 5 decades he can be seen in other shows such as Maude, Barney Miller, Law & Order, and Will and Grace. He also replaced Robert Guillaume on the series Soap after Guillaume left to star in the spinoff Benson.
- Hector Elizondo is probably best known for his television roles on Chicago Hope and most recently Last Man Standing. He can also be seen in such films as The Taking of Pelham One Two Three (1974) and Pretty Woman (1990)

- Eileen Brennan was nominated for Best Supporting Actress for her role in the 1980 feature Private Benjamin and can also be seen in other films such as The Sting (1973), Clue (1985) as well as appearances in numerous television shows.

Edith's Problem 1-8-72
Archie and Edith struggle as she goes through menopause.

Episode notes
- This is the second series appearance for Jeannie Linero (billed here as Jeanie Linero) known for her role in the Godfather.

Archie and the FBI 1-15-72
A Governmental background check throws Archie and his best friend into a state of panic.

Episode notes
- Mike Evans appears again as Lionel Jefferson.

Mike's Mysterious Son 1-22-72
An ex-girlfriend of Mike's drops her son off at the Bunker's claiming Mike is the father.

Episode notes
- The part of Marilyn Sanders is played by Marcia Rodd who would be cast as Maude's daughter Carol in the pilot episode of that series.

Archie Sees a Mugging 1-29-72

Archie fingers the mob when he witnesses a mugging.

Episode notes

- Bill Macy appears as a police officer in this episode. He would go on to co-star with Bea Arthur as her husband Walter in the All in the Family spinoff Maude.

- Ralph Sylvestri is played by Val Bisoglio who is best known to fans of Quincy M.E. as Danny Tovo. He also appeared on such sitcoms as Barney Miller, and M*A*S*H. His final acting roles were in three episodes of the Sopranos in 2002. Bisoglio passed away on October 18, 2021.

- For unknown reasons, there is a slight edit in this episode on the Sony/Shout! Factory DVD set although it was released uncut on VHS through Columbia House in the 1990s.

- Tony Vicino is played by Jack Somack. He would return as Tiny in the season six-episode Archie the Babysitter.

Archie and Edith Alone 2-5-72

With the kids away for a week, Archie and Edith finally have some alone time.

Episode notes

- We learn in this episode that Archie never finished high school and had to quit before his last term to get a job and help the family out.

Edith Gets a Mink 2-12-72

Edith's cousin Amelia gives her a mink coat.

Episode notes

- This is the first appearance of Edith's Cousin Amelia and her husband Russ. They are played in this episode by Rae Allen and Richard Dysart. While Allen will return to the role in season 3, both will be recast when they pay the Bunker's a visit again in season 5.
- Isabel Sanford makes another appearance as Louise Jefferson.

Sammy's Visit 2-19-72

Sammy Davis Jr. leaves his briefcase in Archie's cab and stops by to pick it up.

Episode notes

- Although portraying Barney in the season one episode **Judging Books by Covers**, Billy Halop makes his first appearance as Munson in this episode.
- Allan Melvin makes his first appearance as Barney Heffner in this episode. His wife is named Mabel

in this episode and by the season eight-episode **Unequal Partners**, her name will be changed to Blanche.
- Mike Evans makes another appearance as Lionel Jefferson.
- Isabel Sanford returns as Louise Jefferson.

Edith the Judge 2-26-72
Edith acts as mediary when Archie breaks a washing machine at the local laundromat.

Episode notes
- Jack Weston (Joe Girgis) appeared in many movies and tv shows. Fans of Jerry Lewis will recognize him from "It's Only Money" (1962) but perhaps he is best known to modern audiences as Max Kellerman, the resort proprietor in "Dirty Dancing" (1987)

Archie is Jealous 3-4-72
Archie gets all wound up when he finds out details about a man Edith knew before they were married.

Episode notes
- Brendan Dillon makes another appearance as the Bartender at Kelcy's.

Maude 3-11-72
The Bunkers travel to attend the wedding of Carol Findlay.

Episode notes

- This episode served as the backdoor pilot for Maude which would premiere the following Fall.
- The role of Carol is played by Marcia Rodd who appeared earlier in this season as Marilyn Sanders in the episode **Mike's Mysterious Son**. Adrienne Barbeau would assume the role when the series premiered the following September.
- Bill Macy plays Maude's fourth husband Walter Findlay and would continue in the role when the series went into production. He played an officer in the episode **Archie Sees a Mugging** earlier in season two.
- The repairman is played by All in the Family writer Bernie West.

All in the Family continued as the number one show in America for the 1972-73 series leading CBS's Saturday night lineup. The All in the Family spinoff Maude premiered this season on Monday nights and became the fourth most watched television show of the season while the other Lear co-creation Sanford and Son sat at number two for the end of the year. In a little over a year and a half, Norman Lear was changing the landscape of television.

This is another solid season where staples of the series such as Edith running up to greet Archie upon his return home are established. In several episodes such as **The Locket** and **Edith's Winning Ticket** there is a blend of traditional sitcom plots mixed in with the commentary the series was known for. Archie wants to get ahead even if it involves cheating his fellow man. Several other episodes including **Archie is Branded** and **Gloria the Victim** really shake the format with subject matters that are at times uneasy for the viewer. It is a tribute to the creative forces of the show to put these characters in situations which directly reflected the times and still derive humor from those situations. We are really invested in these characters and we find ourselves laughing and crying along with them while they struggle through the issues at hand. The show punches you in the gut with something which breaks your heart then provides a big laugh to pull you out of it. Many times, you are doing both at once.

At the time the first episode premiered in September, America was on the cusp of a Presidential election with incumbent Richard Nixon battling challenger George McGovern. An Archie Bunker for President campaign was comedically mounted. Archie would not publicly give any speeches in a bid for the White House; however, campaign buttons were produced for fans of the show. Ironically McGovern announced his candidacy days after All in the Family first premiered in 1971. Come election time, it was almost assured that Nixon would be re-elected. McGovern was struggling in the polls so when Mike inherited some money in an episode that premiered just three days before election (**Mike Comes Into Money** aired 11-3-72), he donated it to the McGovern campaign much to Archie's ire. In the summer before this season aired, five men were arrested for breaking into the Democratic National Headquarters at the Watergate Hotel. Ultimately dubbed the "Watergate scandal", the story continued to pick up steam during and after the election. Within a month after the episode aired, the Bunker's – like many American's – were discussing it.

This is one example of how the argument could be made that All in the Family was sometimes too topical and therefore somewhat dates the show. Yet if one would tweak the scripts to adapt to today's political climate, the humor and the humanity would still shine through. The overall themes that the Bunker's dissect week after week; discrimination, equality, violence, racism, politics, sex, and gun control have always been with us and are still prevalent today.

For example, the premiere episode **Archie and the Editorial** addresses the concerns of gun control. The subject was broached in the Bunker household in the season two-episode **Edith Writes a Song** yet here the statistics of the day (which would eventually become television parody fodder as 'very special episodes') are used in counterpoint of Archie favoring private citizens owning handguns. In response to a TV owner's editorial on gun control, Archie goes on TV to provide his counterpoint. To bring some money into the house to help, Gloria gets a job in this episode and to celebrate, takes the family down to Kelsey's for a beer. A short time after they arrive two men enter, one of which recognizes Archie from his appearance on TV. He proceeds to pull a gun on Archie and the two men hold up the bar.

Although she is now working, Gloria continues her struggle to find her voice for female equality which is highlighted across several episodes this season. In **Gloria and the Riddle**, she presents the family with a conundrum to solve about a father and son who are in a car accident. The father is killed and as the son is brought in for surgery, the surgeon says "I can't operate on this boy, he's my son." The answer to the riddle is that the surgeon is a woman yet nobody can provide an answer. Mike condemns his own thinking because he is so conditioned to think of males dominating the professional world. Later in the season, Mike is challenged again in **Mike's Appendix** when he requires an operation. The Bunker's family doctor has referred Mike to Dr. McKenzie yet it will cost more money than a female surgeon Dr. Stern whom Gloria recommends. While Mike continues to advocate in theory for the advancement of women in the United States and the domination of women in some cultures, he personally does not feel comfortable with a woman doctor. The pain becomes too intense and he is brought in for surgery. Archie offers to pay for the surgery and an emotional Gloria struggles to find the words to thank him. The operation is a success and while in recovery, Mike is introduced to Dr. McKenzie who has performed the surgery and as it turns out is a woman. In the final episode of the season **The Battle of the Month**, it is Gloria's birthday and she's received one gift she is not happy with – her period. An argument about female equality erupts between her and Edith and she ends the discussion telling Edith that she is a nobody. There is something in that Bunker blood that makes them verbally attack this poor woman as Archie told Edith she was not human in the previous season's episode **Archie and Edith Alone**. The argument continues well into the night between Gloria and Mike and keeps the whole house up. As it carries downstairs into the Bunker's living room, it is Edith who finally takes charge. She relates a story about her own mother and father and how a seemingly innocent argument over maple syrup caused her parents not to talk for three weeks and how things were never the same afterwards. She reminds Mike and Gloria how much they mean to one another and they make up. Before heading back up to bed, she turns to Edith and says "I'm sorry I called you a nothing, you're really something." It is Edith's calm and loving understanding that continually grounds, guides, and centers the family.

In **The Threat**, Bobbi Jo Loomis – the wife of Archie's old army buddy "the Duke" – comes to stay for the night at the Bunker's. Bobbi Jo is a friendly woman of the South and it is hard for Archie to conceal his attraction to her. To this point in the series, we have only seen the Archie that has been married for 20 plus years but here we see the same Archie that Edith must have when she lovingly describes first meeting him. He cannot handle the combination of arousal and guilt he feels for being attracted to Bobbi Jo as he charms her in a way that is reminiscent of Ralph Kramden in the classic Honeymooners episode "Alice and the Blonde". Instead of dealing with his innocent and yet harmless feelings, he tells the kids that she made a pass at him. Edith overhears this and asks Bobbi Jo to leave the house. Archie tries to do some damage control by justifying what Edith must have heard him say to the kids but it is too late. Bobbi Jo is gone and undoubtedly so is Archie's friendship with "the Duke".

When **Lionel Steps Out**, it is to take the visiting niece of Archie's younger brother Fred out dancing. When Archie finds a picture that Lionel and Linda have taken together, all hell breaks loose. An equally angry Henry Jefferson arrives and both men argue interracial dating but from opposite sides of the fence. We know how Archie feels about this topic but we've yet to address during the series how Edith feels about such matters. When Mike and Gloria inquire, Edith says that her parents always wanted her to date someone who is kind, thoughtful, and a gentleman. Gloria points out that she just described Lionel. That is all Edith needs to hear. Archie demands that he and Lionel talk about this alone. Lionel starts off the conversation by kidding Archie with the usual banter attributed to these two characters. However midway through the discussion, Lionel takes a step back, the tone of his voice changes, and he tells Archie that while he used to get a kick out of him, he is getting older now. While they can continue to be friends Lionel would like Archie to "put a lid" on all his thoughts of black and white / right or wrong. The audience applauds Lionel standing up for himself. It is a significant moment for the two characters as their interactions going forward will no longer be of such an exaggerated nature as they have up to this point. After Lionel leaves, Archie tries to continue the discussion with Linda but she too shuts him down. Archie defends his actions saying that he is protecting her as is his duty to her father. Growing up, Archie says that his brother always wanted to be like him yet he has not seen his brother in over 8 years. When Linda informs him that his brother has changed, Archie reacts with a mixture of anger and sadness. His world has become a little smaller because his brother has evolved while Archie cannot grow and get past his prejudice.

Archie jumps at the chance to become one of the Cannonbowlers in **Archie and the Bowling Team**, sacrificing his relationship with one of his best friends to join this race and faith restricted group. During his tryout, Archie ties with Charlie Green who is a black man yet he feels he is still going to make the team being a white Protestant. Pressure from the league forces the Cannonbowlers to accept Charlie. Although Archie has freely applied his bigotry and racism to others without giving it a second thought, in his mind he feels he is the victim of a changing world around him and cannot understand why. All he can say is "The world's changing and every time it changes it gives me another kick in the butt."

In **The Bunkers and the Swingers**, Edith, feeling lonely around the house since Gloria started work, innocently answers a wife swapping ad thinking the couple is looking for new friends. When the overly friendly Rempley's arrive (portrayed by Vincent Gardenia and Rue McClanahan) the misunderstanding plays out to hilarious results where a confused Archie innocently joins in on the conversation. Once Archie finds out the couple are swingers, he condemns their lifestyle and says they should be ashamed of themselves. Whereas swinging saved the Rempley's from a mundane marriage, the Bunker's lives may be just as mundane yet they have a deep bond and love for one another which keeps them together.

There is a new young kid at Archie's job, Chuck Matthews that Archie fears is after his position. His worry leads to a psychosomatic back condition which lands **Archie in the Hospital**. A stuck partition separates Archie from his roommate, a black man from France named Jean Duval (played by Roscoe Lee Brown) so the two men can only communicate using their words. Archie thinks, of course, that since the man is from France that he must be white. When it is revealed that he is black, Archie's back condition dramatically improves and he checks out of the hospital. Norman Lear said he would have preferred to not reveal the race of the roommate even to the audience so it would challenge our own prejudice yet unfortunately the episode was not shot that way.

Archie is Branded is yet another season episode that deals with violence. In this one, someone has mistakenly painted a swastika on the Bunker's front door. The Bunkers are paid a visit by Paul Benjamin who is with a radical anti-defamation group. A debate ensues about violent vs. non-violent response with Archie on the side of revenge. Mike argues with Paul that he does not want his country committing acts of violence in his name like the way innocent women and children were bombed in Vietnam. Paul counters that the only way the lesson is truly learned is by fighting back using whatever means necessary. Once the mix-up in the houses is discovered, Paul leaves. While the Bunker's banter back and forth about the use of the word "Shalom" we hear an explosion off camera. The family rushes to the door and in a sobering and chilling moment they stand in silence to witness the results of Paul being blown up in his car.

Everybody Tells the Truth revisits a classic television premise (in such shows as the Dick Van Dyke episode "The Night the Roof Fell In") where each character recounts an event according to how they remember things happening. In this episode, it is the story of a visit earlier in the day by a refrigerator repairman. In each character's version of the story, they portray themselves how they think they act and portray others as they see them, very much like most of us do in real life. Arguably, it may be the definitive episode of the series. In the end, it is no surprise that

Edith is the sole observer who sees the events closest to how they really happened. When Archie refers to the repairman's assistant as "boy", he is immediately corrected by saying "I'm not a boy, I'm a man." Archie responds that he is as well but he does not have to make a 'pernt' of it. The assistant retorts "You've never had to make a *point* of it." For a moment, we see Archie with his defenses down and realizing that he has said something wrong yet will not outwardly admit it. He clumsily recovers and uncomfortably thanks the repairman for coming and tells them he can finish the job for them and they can leave. In an episode filled with exaggerated characterizations, it is a subtle and poignant moment. The execution is brilliant in this episode and displays just how in command these actors are of their roles.

Regarding the support of the cast to the overall presentation of the material, Norman Lear recalled "we as writers would come in time and again to see a rehearsal of a script we wrote and find a group of inventions that we hadn't seen on paper that the actors and director found in rehearsal"[34] Rob Reiner continued "Carroll created a creative atmosphere amongst the cast to allow us to contribute.... the actors would give notes to each other and to the writers. Everybody was allowed to participate."[35]

Archie is up for a dispatcher job but as we have learned before, he never finished high school. He goes back to night school for his diploma in **Archie Learns His Lesson**. Edith explains to the kids what happened with Archie while he was growing up and why he never finished school. She also tells them the story about the origin of the word dingbat. Archie was shy when they were dating and was uncomfortable saying words like sweetheart so he came up with the word dingbat. No matter how many times Edith hears dingbat she hears a little sweetheart in there too. Archie succeeds in getting his diploma yet misses out on the job to the owner's nephew.

Gloria is attacked in the episode **Gloria the Victim**. Upon coming home, she turns to Edith for support. Edith consoles Gloria but struggles when listening to the details because she does not want to hear about what she knows has happened. While she comforts Gloria, she continues to tell her an inane story about her day to keep the moment as normal as possible. When Archie demands they catch this man, he calls the police. When the Detective comes over, he paints a not too pretty picture of what might happen if it went to trial. Gloria wants no part of it but a further conversation where Edith relates a story from her younger days when she was almost attacked changes her mind. When she comes back in and says she wants to pursue, it is Archie and Mike who wind up talking her out of it again. While Mike may rally and protest for the injustices to a world of strangers, he will not extend the same to his own wife to 'protect' her. As the episode ends

Archie says that they took care of their own today as the camera closes in on Gloria who is visibly shaking.

All the principles were nominated for their roles this season along with John Rich and Bob LaHendro for their directorial efforts in **The Bunkers and the Swingers** but would go home empty handed. The series again won for Outstanding Comedy Series. The episode **The Bunkers and the Swingers** won for Outstanding Writing Achievement for Norman Lear, Michael Ross, and Bernie West. The series also took home Golden Globes for Best TV Show and Best TV Actress for Jean Stapleton. The rest of the cast received nominations but no wins.

season three episodes

Archie and the Editorial 9-16-72
After disagreeing with a station managers editorial on gun control, Archie goes on the air to state his rebuttal.

Episode notes
- actor Sorrell Brooke appears in this episode as the station manager. He is best known for his portrayal as Boss Hogg on The Dukes of Hazzard.
- Mike Evans makes another appearance as Lionel Jefferson.

- Brendan Dillon makes an appearance as the bartender at Kelcy's
- beginning with this episode, Carroll O'Connor shares a co-writing credit with Roger Kellaway for the closing theme Remembering You as O'Connor added lyrics to the, up to that point, instrumental piece.

Archie's Fraud 9-23-72

When threatened with tax fraud for not reporting his tips from driving the cab, Archie visits the IRS to straighten things out.

Episode notes

- this episode is reminiscent of Archie's distant television relative Ralph Kramden who tangled with the IRS in the classic Honeymooners episode "The Worry Wart".
- Billy Halop makes an appearance as Munson.
- James McEachin plays the part of the tax examiner. McEachin can be seen as a guest on such shows as The Wild Wild West, The Rockford Files, Murder, She Wrote and as a recurring character in the 80s/90s revival of Perry Mason. The actor will return to All in the Family in season seven.

The Threat 9-30-72

The wife of Archie's army buddy comes to stay the night at the Bunker's house.

Episode notes

- this is the first episode to feature the set for the Bunker's bedroom.
- Archie makes note that he was with the 15th air corps during World War II.
- Bobbi Jo Loomis is played by Gloria LeRoy. She will return to the series as Mildred "Boom Boom" Turner in season five and would star in the Norman Lear series Hot L Baltimore which ran for a single season in 1975.

Gloria and the Riddle 10-7-72

Gloria presents a riddle to the family that they cannot figure out.

Episode notes

- Allan Melvin makes an appearance as Barney.
- Brendan Dillon makes his final appearance as the bartender at Kelcy's.

Lionel Steps Out 10-14-72

Archie loses it when he finds out his visiting niece is going out dancing with Lionel.

Episode notes
- Edith mentions she has a brother Harry.
- Edith also mentions that her father died a year before she met Archie.
- When Edith tries to hide the picture from Archie, he questions if she is going through 'the change' again.
- Mel Stewart returns as Henry Jefferson.
- While Archie's brother is named Fred in this episode, he is named Phil in the season two episode **The Saga of Cousin Oscar**.
- Archie's niece Linda says that her father raised four girls. While we never see Linda again, we will meet Linda's sister Billie in the season three premiere of Archie Bunker's Place.
- Mike Evans makes an appearance as Lionel Jefferson.

Edith Flips Her Wig 10-21-72
When Edith absent-mindedly leaves a department store wearing a wig she did not pay for, she fears she is a kleptomaniac.

Episode notes
- Barnard Hughes makes his second appearance as Father John Majeski.

The Bunkers and the Swingers 10-28-72

Edith innocently answers a wife swapping ad feeling the couple is just lonely and would like new friends.

Episode notes

- Vincent Gardinia returns to the series as Curtis Rempley. He will be added to the recurring cast as Frank Lorenzo in season four.
- Rue McClanahan who plays Ruth Rempley was concurrently appearing on Maude (1972-1978) and would go on to greater fame as Blanche Deveraux (with Maude co-star Bea Arthur) in the classic sitcom The Golden Girls (1985-1992). She would reprise the role of Blanche in the single season spin-off The Golden Palace.
- Isabel Sanford makes an appearance as Louise Jefferson.
- look closely when Edith takes the pie crust out of the oven. She has one yellow and one red potholder yet when they filmed the closeup insert, the potholders are reversed from the master shot.

Mike Comes Into Money 11-4-72

Mike decides to use his inheritance money to donate to the McGovern campaign.

Flashback: Mike and Gloria's Wedding (part I) 11-11-72

Flashback: Mike and Gloria's Wedding (part II) 11-18-72

The family reminisces about Mike and Gloria's wedding day.

Episode notes

- These episodes were co-written by Rob Reiner
- Although in the episode **Now That You Know the Way Let's Be Strangers**, Paul Goodrow is said to have been Mike's best man at their wedding he is nowhere to be found in this episode.
- Mike mentions that both his parents died when he was young.
- This is the first episode where the running gag "Reverend Fletcher, Feltcher, whatever" is used.
- In the flashback sequence Lionel tells Archie he wants to be an electrical engineer which is a nod back to the pilot episode.
- The part of Mike's Uncle Casimir is played by movie and TV veteran Michael Conrad, best known for his role as Sgt. Phil Esterhuas on the groundbreaking drama Hill Street Blues.
- Mike Evans makes an appearance as Lionel Jefferson in part II of the story.
- Peggy Rea appears (unbilled) as a wedding guest in part two. Rea previously portrayed cousin Bertha in the season one-episode **The Saga of Cousin Oscar** and earlier in the season two-episode **The Blockbuster**. She will return as Edith's friend Martha

Birkhorn in the season nine-episode **Barney, the Gold Digger**.

Mike's Appendix 12-2-72

Mike is rushed to the hospital to have his appendix removed.

Episode notes

- according to this episode, it cost about $350 for an appendix operation back in 1972.

Edith's Winning Ticket 12-9-72

Archie tries to figure a way to swindle the Jeffersons out of a $500 winning sweepstakes ticket Edith purchased for them.

Episode notes

- Mel Stewart makes a return appearance as Henry Jefferson.
- Isabel Sanford appears as Louise Jefferson.
- Although Archie and Edith discuss that there is no problem with a little gambling, a later episode will deal with the story that Archie at one time battled a gambling addiction.

Archie and the Bowling Team 12-16-72

Archie has an opportunity to join the Cannonbowlers, a restricted bowling group.

Episode notes
- Allen Melvin appears in this episode as Barney Hefner.
- If you look closely to the right as Barney leaves the house, you will catch a glimpse of one of the cameras in the shot.

The Locket 12-23-72
Edith misplaces a family heirloom and Archie tries to swindle the insurance money for a new television set.

Episode notes
- This episode was co-written by Arthur Marx, son of legendary comedian Groucho Marx. He would go on to pen episodes of The Paul Lynde Show, The Jeffersons, Maude, and Alice.
- One of the delivery men that Archie stiffs with a 50-cent tip is Louis Guss. He will return to collect in season eight when he portrays Sam, who robs Archie's Place in the episode **Archie and the Super Bowl**.

Archie in the Hospital 1-6-73
Archie takes on symptoms of a backache when he worries about losing his job to a young newcomer.

Episode notes
- Mike Evans appears as Lionel Jefferson

- Isabel Sanford makes another appearance as Louise Jefferson
- The part of the nurse is played by Priscilla Morrill who made other appearances on shows like Mary Tyler Moore and Maude. She will return to All in the Family in various roles.

Oh Say Can You See 1-20-73

Archie struggles with getting older after running into an old high school classmate.

Episode notes
- The part of Bill Mulheron is played by Larry Storch who has appeared in close to 250 television shows both as a performer and voice actor. He is probably best known for his role as Corporal Agarn in the 1965 series F-Troop.
- Bob Hastings returns behind the bar at Kelcy's although his character is spelled "Kelsey" in the closing credits.
- Arlene Golonka plays Tina and co-starred with Ken Berry in the Andy Griffith Show spinoff Mayberry RFD. She also appeared in an episode of M*A*S*H playing accident prone nurse Edwina Ferguson.

Archie Goes Too Far 1-27-73

After violating Mike's privacy and reading a poem he wrote to another woman before meeting Gloria, the family walks out on him in protest.

Episode notes

- While she has been mentioned before, this is the first time we meet Gloria's girlfriend Trudy (played by Pamela Murphy). The next time we see her will be in the season six-episode **New Year's Wedding** when she will be portrayed by a different actor.
- Betty Sue is played by Mary Kay Place who has had a long career in everything from M*A*S*H to Big Love, writing (M*A*S*H and The Mary Tyler Moore Show), and directing (Friends and Arli$$)
- Mike Evans appears as Lionel Jefferson.

Class Reunion 2-10-73

Edith takes a reluctant Archie to her 30th class reunion.

Episode notes

- Priscilla Morrill returns as one of Edith's former classmates.
- Film and television veteran Harvey Lembeck co-stars in this episode. He appeared in Stalag 17 and as Eric Von Zipper in the beach party movies of the 1960s in addition to countless other roles. Among several other television appearances, he was on Batman, The Monkees, and The Partridge Family.
- Bernie Hamilton guests in this episode and is probably best known as Captain Doby from the hit 70s series Starsky and Hutch.
- Cousin Amelia is again portrayed by Rae Allen.

The Hot Watch 2-17-72

Archie buys a stolen watch off a guy down at the dock.

Episode notes

- Mike Evans appears as Lionel Jefferson.

Archie is Branded 2-24-73

A swastika is mistakenly painted on the Bunker's door.

Episode notes

- The part of Paul Benjamin is played by veteran actor Gregory Sierra who would go on to portray Detective Chano Amenguale in the first two seasons of Barney Miller along with dozens of other film and television appearances. Sierra passed away on January 4, 2021.

Everybody Tells the Truth 3-3-73

Mike and Archie both recount their experiences earlier in the day with a refrigerator repairman and his assistant.

Episode notes

- The restaurant set is the same used in the previous season episode **The Elevator Story** only this time it is French and not Italian.
- This was the first television appearance for Ron Glass who plays the repairman's helper Jack. Glass would go on to star as Detective Ron Harris in the classic sitcom Barney Miller. More recently

he starred in the cult sci-fi classic Firefly and made guest appearances on various television shows before his passing on November 25, 2016.
- Ken Lynch makes his second and final appearance in the series as Bob the repairman.

Archie Learns His Lesson 3-10-73
Needing his high school diploma for a promotion, Archie goes back to night school.

Gloria the Victim 3-17-73
Gloria is attacked on her way home from work.

Episode notes
- Veteran character actor Charles Durning appears as the Detective in this episode. It was his second television appearance. The dependable character actor appeared in countless feature films including the 1975 classic Dog Day Afternoon. Among his final work was a recurring role on the Denis Leary series Rescue Me. Durning passed away on Christmas Eve in 2012.
- We learn in this episode that the Jeffersons have a dog named Wilma yet you never see or hear about her again.
- During the investigation, a reference is made to the season two-episode **Gloria Poses in the Nude** where Gloria posed for her and Mike's friend Szabo.

- Edith tells the Detective that she was once on a jury in a reference to the episode **Edith Has Jury Duty** from season one.
- Mike Evans makes a return appearance as Lionel Jefferson.
- Mel Stewart returns as Henry Jefferson

The Battle of the Month 3-24-73

Gloria is suffering from PMS on her birthday and gets in a fight with Edith.

Episode notes

- It is mentioned in this episode that Archie once lost his whole paycheck in a poker game. This theme will be explored again in season four.

To the modern television viewer, the term 'Must See TV' conjures up memories of shows such as Seinfeld and Friends.

In 1972, M*A*S*H, based on the hit 1970 feature film by Robert Altman, debuted to low ratings on CBS. It was on the brink of cancellation when the wife of then President Bob Wood expressed her love for the show so it was given another shot. For season two, M*A*S*H was placed behind All in the Family on the Saturday night schedule and went on to become one of the most beloved series in television history. Followed by The Mary Tyler Moore Show, The Bob Newhart Show, and The Carol Burnett Show, this lineup has gone down as one of the greatest in television history.

Norman Lear continued to break ground with yet another spin-off this season. Co-created by Mike Evans, Good Times premiered in February of 1974. It told the story of the Evans family who lived in the projects of Chicago. The matriarch of the family Florida Evans (played by Esther Rolle) had been the maid of Edith's cousin Maude during the first two seasons of that spinoff. John Amos appeared as Florida's husband James in a handful of episodes and because they had such strong chemistry, he was brought over to the series as it started production. Standup comic Jimmy Walker was cast as their eldest child J.J. and the show became another smash for Lear.

Whereas most episodes up to this point are framed around Archie's bigotry and prejudice to drive the comedy and story, those elements take more of a backseat as this season progresses. Like season three, in episodes such as **Archie Eats and Runs** and the season finale **Mike's Graduation**, the humor evolves from situations more akin to classic sitcoms than from many of the themes which dominate the first three seasons of the series. Relationships are explored with more depth and these story lines remain well-crafted half hours of television.

It's business as usual however in the season opener with the two-parter **We're Having a Heat Wave / We're Still Having a Heat Wave** where amid arguing with Mike over Nixon's involvement in Watergate (Nixon would resign from office almost a year after this episode originally aired), Archie once again is involved with a petition to keep minorities off the block as he had in **The First and Last Supper** from season one. Archie finds a strange bedfellow in Henry Jefferson when they unite over concern of who might be buying a house for sale on the block. Even Henry signs the petition. It turns out to be a Puerto Rican couple whom Archie lies to about the condition of the house. This scares them away although they find a bigger house for the same money on the next block. With the house available again, it is sold to Frank and Irene Lorenzo.

Veteran stage actor Vincent Gardenia was no stranger to All in the Family, appearing in two previous episodes including the Emmy winning **The Bunkers and the Swingers** and was brought on to play the role of the new neighbor Frank Lorenzo. Gardenia grew restless with the role and quietly disappeared from the cast after six appearances. His wife Irene was played by Betty Garrett, known to MGM musical fans for her work in such films as Take Me Out to the Ballgame and On the Town (both 1949). After her work on All in the Family, she would go on to portray Edna Babish DeFazio on the 1970's series Laverne & Shirley. Garrett knew O'Connor as a serious person from their early days together working in the theatre and was amazed at his transformation with the Archie Bunker character. "He caught the fact that the person was a human being which I think is better than just making him an out and out villain....I think we have to understand that some of the villains are charming and have feelings too. What's dangerous about them is that we get hooked into their charm without realizing how bigoted they are."[36] Garrett recalled in 2003. The Lorenzo's are an interesting couple by 1973 standards; Frank has an ambiguous sales job of some sort, is semi-retired, and loves to cook. Irene on the other hand is independent, handy with tools, and worst of all for Archie, a Catholic. With the Jeffersons storylines somewhat exhausted, this gives Archie the opportunity to spar with some new adversaries who threaten his way of life.

Since Gloria took a job in season three, Edith has been lonely around the house and her points of reference to current affairs are television shows such as Mannix and Marcus Welby M.D. After meeting Irene, she really bonds with her at one point admitting "I know you're not a movie star or nothin' but I think I'm gettin' to be a fan of yours." Irene encourages Edith to grow as an independent woman and the time they spend together helps Edith to find her voice and clearly makes Archie insecure. When Edith decides to broaden her horizons and check out Irene's religion (**Edith's Conversion**), Archie is worried that she will want to become a Catholic. As the season unfolds, with Irene's influence Edith stands up more to Archie and finds a stronger voice in their relationship. Archie is not so quick to shout her down anymore as he may have done in the past. He is becoming more willing to give in as the experiences and influences around him continue to chip away at his out of touch attitudes.

Edith Finds an Old Man features actor Burt Mustin as an elderly man that Edith finds at Ferguson's Market and brings home. Mustin made a late start in acting when he made his television debut at age 67 and played Harry Feeny in the season one episode **Archie is Worried About His Job**. Classic TV fans will also recognize him as Gus the Fireman from Leave it to Beaver and he guested on everything from The Abbott and Costello Show to the Twilight Zone. Here he plays Mr. Justin Quigley who has been placed in a retirement home and is all but forgotten by his family. While staying with the Bunkers, Quigley places a call to his friend Joe to come pick him. Worried about another "freeloader" in the house, Archie feels the Government should take care of him and it is not his responsibility to do so. Mike reminds him that a social security payout is below what the poverty level is. When Joe finally shows up at the house, it is really Jo - a woman - who proceeds to take Quigley home with her so they can live together. For a couple even older than Archie, they are more enlightened to the times. It is about survival for them than anything else as if they were to get married, Jo would lose half of her social security. Before they leave, Quigley gives Archie one piece of advice, not to get old. When Archie asks what that means, Quigley replies "You'll find out."

When Archie arrives home, bestowing presents on his family and says "Lady luck shined on me today," Edith knows he has been gambling again in **Archie and the Gambler**. In this episode we learn that Archie had a gambling addiction when they first got married. The addiction was so bad that at one point Archie lost the family car in a bet and Edith was going to leave him. Edith calls it 'the sickness' and when she receives a phone call that Archie's placed another bet after promising her it was a onetime thing, she slaps him across the face. She feels remorse while Archie hides out at Kelcy's Bar. After being encouraged by his buddies to stand up for himself, he returns home demanding an apology. Edith reads him an apology note only it is the note that Archie wrote to her early on in their marriage when he first struggled with his addiction. Archie says that is so old it has expired yet according to Edith; all he needs to do is update it with his signature and date. While he is signing, all Archie can say is "You're a pip Edith, a real pip."

In **Henry's Farewell**, Henry Jefferson leaves the neighborhood to open a cleaning store and work with his brother George. Behind the scenes, the actor playing Henry Jefferson (Mel Stewart) went on to co-star in Roll Out an ill-fated M*A*S*H inspired sitcom which aired for half a season on CBS. In this episode, we are finally introduced to his brother George whom we have only heard about up to this point. Sherman Hemsley (born February 1, 1938) was another stage actor whom Norman Lear recruited and was hired for the part of George Jefferson. Hemsley was originally going to debut on the series back in season one but was reluctant to leave the stage. The introduction of George is clever in that we do not see him at first, we only hear him yelling at Archie from behind the front door of the Bunker house. Once he is let in, we learn that George is every bit as prejudiced and bigoted as Archie. George and Archie will bond for a moment later in the season in **Lionel's Engagement,** when Lionel announces his engagement to Jenny Willis. George protests loudly when he discovers that her father is white. Louise accepts a dance from Mr. Willis and the party goes on. A defeated George staggers back to the bar where he meets an equally disappointed Archie. In their one scene of solidarity, they toast one another as Archie says "Here's to yesterday."

In **Archie and the Computer** Edith sends in a 25-cent rebate coupon to a prune company and because of a computer error continues to receive quarters in the mail. Archie does not want it to stop ("You found the goose that laid the golden prune!" he exclaims) and has no trouble trying to influence her to say nothing so the money will keep coming in. While Archie supports computers doing the work of humans when it benefits him, he changes his tune when Edith receives a letter from the Veterans Administration notifying her, because of a computer glitch, that Archie is deceased. In a somewhat prophetic observation and commentary, Mike says that soon we will no longer be names, just numbers and that there is no more human contact as the whole country is being ruled by machines.

Archie fares a little better financially, for the moment, in **The Taxi Caper**. While moonlighting for Munson, he is held up and his wallet containing $50 is stolen. After filing a report with the police, it turns out that the thief is the son of a local politician. Archie is visited by an attorney who pays him $100 to retract his story. When the thief is caught, Archie goes down to the station and says he no longer wants to press charges. His wallet has been recovered but the money is gone. Plus, his cab was parked illegally and in addition to the $25 ticket, it will cost him $50 to get it out of the pound. Archie winds up $25 in the hole and the thief, whose robbery of Archie was his third offense, remains free to do it again. Archie believes in supporting the law and local law enforcement unless he can make a couple of bucks off if it.

Where it is usually Archie's bigotry and prejudice that are under the microscope, it is Mike's behavior that is examined in **The Games Bunkers Play**. For years, Mike has lived under Archie's roof and on Archie's dime yet time and time again, feels superior and denounces the very hand that is feeding him. In this episode, Mike has a new board game called Group Therapy and has invited the neighbors over to play. Archie does not want any part of it and leaves. Mike thinks this will be a perfect opportunity for total honesty as well as taking several pot shots at Archie all while holding court in Archie's chair and becoming every bit as obnoxious. As the game unfolds,

80

Mike's own arrogance and shortcomings are exposed, even by Lionel who somewhat defends Archie saying he behaves the way he does because he doesn't know any better. Mike angrily overturns the board and storms upstairs. When he sheepishly returns, it is Edith who takes him aside to explain that Archie does not hate him but is jealous of him because of all the opportunities Mike has. "Edith had a way of bottom lining something that you knew exactly what she was getting at"[37] recalled Sally Struthers. When Mike is left alone to absorb Edith's comments, Archie returns home and Mike embraces him saying "I understand." The episode reveals that even Mike, for all his education and awareness with society (provided it is disconnected from his life), can be a little hypocritical in his own behavior just like Archie and there is some common ground seen between the two men. It is Mike who has probably learned the most valuable lesson about himself by playing a game he encouraged others to play so he could learn about them.

Archie in the Cellar is a tour de force for Carroll O'Connor who flies solo for most of this episode. With the rest of the family gone for the weekend, Archie is left alone and accidentally locks himself in the cellar. He finds a bottle of Polish Vodka, courtesy of Mike's Uncle Casimir, and proceeds to get drunk. Once inebriated, he feels he is going to die and starts to record his last will and "tentacle", hallucinating conversations with Edith, Mike, and Gloria along the way. When the oil man comes to the house, Archie believes it is Jesus coming to take him. As the oil man makes his way through the house and down to the cellar, he turns out to be an African-American man. Archie bows to him and says "Forgive me Lord…the Jeffersons was right" in reference to the season one episode **The First and Last Supper** where Archie and Henry argued that God was black. The single character monolog driven theme would be used again in an episode of Maude ("The Analyst") and M*A*S*H ("Hawkeye").

Gloria continues to grow into more confident woman. When **Mike and Gloria Mix it Up,** the kids are left home when Archie and Edith go out for the evening in a somewhat reworking of the season two-episode **Archie and Edith Alone**. Gloria decides to take the role of the aggressor in their relationship and makes advances toward Mike which make him uncomfortable. Mike believes that the man should make the move, not the woman and an argument ensues not unlike one Archie would have with Edith. They both storm out of the house and go their separate ways. When they return, they each make up a story about meeting someone which supports their individual points of view. As it turns out that they both went to the same movie, miserable about the fight that has happened and make up. Once again, whereas Mike champions equality to the masses, he still struggles with it personally. In **Gloria Sings the Blues,** she is worried that she has fallen out of love with Michael and takes it out on Archie and Edith saying she does not want to end up like them. After thinking it over, she sits with Edith who explains that she had the same fear once in her relationship with Archie and that it is completely normal. Edith philosophizes that maybe divorces happen because people do not wait long enough to recognize each other again.

It is another emotional Holiday for the Bunkers this season in **Edith's Christmas Story** when Edith reveals that she has a lump in her breast. It was an issue that Stapleton did not want dramatized. She related her initial discomfort in an interview with the Archive of American Television recalling "we had a little talk and (Lear) said 'well it's not about breast cancer, it's about love and how she's providing for the family and comforting them' and I said oh of course and so I was able to do it with pleasure and ease and peace."[38] In the episode, Edith worries that if she has to have a mastectomy that she will change and be different for Archie. Irene calms her and reveals that she herself had the same surgery years ago and it never affected her marriage, reassuring Edith that Archie loves her no matter what. When Archie discovers she has gone to the hospital to have the lump tested, he rushes to her side. While the lump was benign and has been removed, she still must stay overnight in the hospital. When she found out she did not have cancer, she excitedly jumped off the examining table and broke her ankle!

Archie and Edith celebrate their 25th wedding anniversary in the episode **Second Honeymoon**. Edith surprises Archie with an overnight stay at the Hotel Atlantic City, the same hotel they stayed at on their wedding night however Archie has a ticket to the Lakers / Knicks game that weekend. Edith puts Archie in his place and tells him they are going. When they arrive, Archie would rather watch The Three Stooges on the late show but Edith insists they sit and talk. When she excuses herself to change for bed, she comes out wearing a very elegant nightgown. The kids have sent them a bottle of champagne and Archie finally melts when he lays his eyes on her. She proposes a toast thanking him for twenty-five years of marriage. He responds that he could not have done it without her and they embrace and kiss. For a show that is normally at a high decibel level, it is another quiet moment in the series that demonstrates the deep love and understanding that Archie and Edith and have for one another.

Gloria has befriended George, a boy with special needs who works as a box boy at Ferguson's Market in **Gloria's Boyfriend**. Archie tries to do the right things by giving him direction and insisting he stay at the house and take a break from his job. While Archie tries to use a plane that does not seem to be working correctly to trim a door that is sticking, George offers to look at the tool. It is expected that Archie will always say the wrong things yet in this episode, much of the humor falls flat and is not received very well by the audience as it is done at the expense of someone who is defenseless. When George realizes that Archie is making fun of him, he storms out of the house insisting that he will "show them all." His worried father shows up informing the Bunkers that George has lost his job at Ferguson's and has not seen him all afternoon. George returns having found another job and shows Archie a picture that his grade school teacher gave him which has the quote "Every Man is my superior in that I may learn from him." George tells Archie that anyone can learn from anyone and proceeds to fix the plane; Archie had the blade in backwards!

The season closes with the episode **Mike's Graduation** and Archie is so excited for Mike's final exams, he's resorted to calling him Michael and is eager to turn their bedroom into his den. While it appears for a moment that Mike and Gloria will be leaving, Mike is offered an opportunity to enter a master's program. This extends the Stivic's stay with Archie one more season yet it would be the star of the series himself who would soon, amid script disapproval, salary disputes, and creative control, threaten not to return to the number one show on television.

Director John Rich, who was responsible for the directing chores on the majority of the first 85 episodes of the series (and producing seasons three and four) left at the conclusion of season four. He would go on to direct episodes for the series' Benson and the one season All in the Family inspired show Condo. Bob La Hendro who served as associate director the first four years departed as well and would move on to direct episodes of That's My Mama, Welcome Back, Kotter, and the short-lived Hot L Baltimore which was created by Norman Lear.

The series and all four actors were again nominated for the Emmy's in 1974 yet Rob Reiner was the only one to bring home an award. Jean Stapleton received a Golden Globe and the series was named best of the year.

season four episodes

We're Having a Heat Wave 9-15-73
We're Still Having a Heat Wave 9-22-73
The Bunker's battle the energy crisis during a heat wave while Archie and Henry conspire to keep a Puerto Rican family from moving into the neighborhood. Meanwhile Frank and Irene Lorenzo move into the house.

Episode notes
- Clara Weidermeyer last paid a visit to the Bunker's in season one and it is her and her husband's house that is being sold in this episode.
- Vincent Gardenia makes his first appearance as Frank Lorenzo in this episode. He can also be seen in the feature films Bang the Drum Slowly

(1973) with Robert DeNiro and as Cher's father in Moonstruck (1987) both of which would garner him a best supporting actor nomination. He previously guest starred as Jim Bowman in the season one episode **Lionel Moves Into the Neighborhood** and as Curtis Rempley in **The Bunkers and the Swingers** from season three.
- Betty Garrett makes her first appearance as Irene Lorenzo
- Mel Stewart returns as Henry Jefferson in this episode.
- The "Goddamn it!" exchange is the last bit of dialog which was rescued from the original pilot episode script for ABC.

Edith Finds an Old Man 9-29-73
Edith brings home an old man she found wandering the parking lot at Ferguson's Market.

Episode notes
- this is the first episode to feature Burt Mustin as Mr. Justin Quigley. Mustin also appeared on All in the Family in the season one episode **Archie is Worried About His Job**.
- Jo is played by Ruth McDevitt may be best known for the 1963 Alfred Hitchcock classic The Birds.
- Gloria notes that she never knew her Grandparents and asks Mr. Quigley and Jo if they would be her Grandparents.

Archie and the Kiss 10-6-73

When a replica of Rodin's 'the Kiss' is gifted to Gloria, Archie takes it upon himself to give it back.

Episode notes
- Vincent Gardenia and Betty Garrett return as Frank and Irene Lorenzo.
- We learn in this episode that the Lorenzo's have two sons yet we will never meet them.

Archie the Gambler 10-13-73

Archie bets money on a horse and Edith fears he will start gambling again.

Episode notes
- It is revealed in this episode that the first song Archie and Edith danced to was Blue Moon.
- Bob Hastings makes an appearance as Kelsey.
- Allan Melvin returns in this episode as Barney.

Henry's Farewell 10-20-73

The Bunker's throw a farewell party for Henry Jefferson who is moving to work with his brother George at one of his cleaning stores.

Episode notes
- Vincent Gardenia appears as Frank Lorenzo
- Mike Evans makes another appearance as Lionel Jefferson.

- Isabel Sanford returns as Louise Jefferson
- Mel Stewart makes his final appearance as Henry Jefferson.
- Sherman Helmsley makes his first appearance as George Jefferson.

Archie and the Computer 10-27-73

Edith continues to receive quarters in the mail due to a computer glitch after sending in a 25-cent rebate to a prune company.

Episode notes

- Jack Grimes makes his second and final appearance as funeral director Mr. Whitehead.

The Games Bunkers Play 11-3-73

Mike wants the group to play a board game but soon resents everyone when he feels he is being attacked.

Episode notes
- Vincent Gardenia and Betty Garret appear as Frank and Irene Lorenzo
- Mike Evans returns as Lionel Jefferson.

Edith's Conversion 11-10-73

Archie worries that Edith wants to convert to Catholicism.

Episode notes

- Barnard Hughes makes his third and final appearance in this episode as Father John Majeski.

Archie in the Cellar 11-17-73

With the family gone for the weekend, Archie accidentally locks himself in the cellar.

Episode notes

- Betty Garrett makes a brief appearance as Irene Lorenzo in this episode.
- This is the first time in the series we hear Archie tell Edith that he loves her, only he is having a hallucination that is he seeing her at the time he says it.
- The part of the furnace man is played by Juan DeCarlos. He will return to the series in the season seven episode **The Boarder Patrol**.

Black is the Color of My True Love's Wig 11-24-73

Mike shows some renewed interest in Gloria after she purchases a black wig.

Second Honeymoon 12-1-73

Archie and Edith go to Atlantic City to celebrate their 25th wedding anniversary.

Episode notes

- Isabel Sanford appears as Louise Jefferson.
- Archie and Edith stayed in room 822 of the Hotel Atlantic City and Edith gets the same room to celebrate in this episode.
- A ticket to see a Lakers / Knicks game in 1973 would set you back $7.50!

The Taxi Caper 12-8-73

Archie is robbed in his cab and is persuaded to drop the charges after accepting a bribe for his silence.

Episode notes

- In one scene after Archie returns from the police station, a microphone can be seen in the upper frame of the screen.
- Detective Roselli is played by Michael Pataki who had a long career in film and television. Happy Days fans will recognize him as Count Malachi. He will return to All in the Family in the season seven-episode **Archie's Chair**.
- Actor Robert Mandan who appears as Mr. Morrison is perhaps best known as Chester Tate in the series Soap.

Archie is Cursed 12-15-73

Archie bets Irene on a game of pool not knowing she is somewhat of an expert. To save face he pretends to throw out his back after Frank puts a curse on him.

Episode notes

- Vincent Gardenia and Betty Garrett appear again as Frank and Irene Lorenzo
- Sherman Hemsley returns as George Jefferson.
- Bob Hastings makes another appearance as Kelsey.
- When the partition is pulled back in Kelcy's Bar, it reveals a pool table in the next room yet later in the

series, that area will be the site of the storeroom / office and bathrooms.

Edith's Christmas Story 12-22-73
Edith discovers a lump on her breast and fears she has cancer.

Episode notes
- This is the final appearance of Vincent Gardenia as Frank Lorenzo.
- Betty Garrett returns as Irene Lorenzo.

Mike and Gloria Mix it Up 1-5-74
Mike and Gloria spend the evening alone and Mike feels uncomfortable about Gloria being the aggressor in their relationship.

Episode notes
- When the second act of the show begins, the lights are off in the Bunker's house even though the kids did not shut them off when they left at the end of the first act.

Archie Feels Left Out 1-12-74
Archie has anxiety about turning 50 years old and tries to convince everyone that he is 49.

Episode notes
- Burt Mustin returns as Mr. Quigley.
- Ruth McDevitt appears as Jo.

- Betty Garrett makes another appearance as Irene Lorenzo.
- Mike Evans returns as Lionel Jefferson.
- Isabel Sanford appears again as Louise Jefferson.
- Bob Hastings returns as Kelsey.
- When Archie mentions that having another birthday reminds him of all the things he has not done such as riding a horse, getting his picture in the paper, or eating Oysters Rockefeller, he seems to forget that he was on TV twice (even though Richard E. Nixon pre-empted one of his appearances).

Et Tu, Archie 1-26-74
Archie feels threatened that an old friend is going to take his job.

Episode notes
- Joe Tucker is played by Vic Tayback who guested in many TV series such as The Monkees and The Partridge Family. He is best known as Mel Sharples, the owner of Mel's Diner in the series Alice (1976-1985)
- We find out in this episode that Joe Tucker had a nickname for Archie down at work – meathead!
- The Personnel Manager is played by David Doyle, better known to Charlie's Angles fans as Mr. Bosley.

Gloria's Boyfriend 2-2-74
Gloria befriends a man with special needs who is a box boy at Ferguson's Market.

Episode notes

- The part of George is played by Richard Masur who would play Ann Romano's boyfriend David Kane on the Norman Lear produced One Day at a Time (1975-1984). More recently he was a guest star on the Netflix series Orange is the New Black.
- The quote "Every man is my superior in that I may learn from him" is attributed both to Scottish writer Thomas Carlyle and American author Ralph Waldo Emerson.

Lionel's Engagement 2-8-74

Lionel announces his engagement to Jenny Willis without telling his parent's that her father is white.

Episode notes

- Sherman Hemsley, Isabel Sanford, and Mike Evans all reprise their roles as The Jeffersons.
- Zara Cully makes her first appearance as Mother Jefferson and would continue the role until her death in 1978.
- Lynne Moody plays Jenny Willis although she will be recast when The Jeffersons spin-off on their own series.
- The parts of Helen and Tom (here named Louis) Willis are played by Kim Hamilton and Charles Aidman. They will be recast as well with Roxie Roker and Franklin Cover assuming the roles.

Archie Eats and Runs 2-16-74

Archie rushes for emergency treatment after he fears the mushrooms he just ate might be poisoned.

Episode notes

- The nurse played by Jane Dulo may be best remembered from the series McHale's Navy (where she co-starred with fellow All in the Family guest star Bob Hastings)
- Richard Stahl makes his second appearance on the show playing the part of the doctor.
- Archie's mother's maiden name was Longstreet.
- Archie's social security number is 129-14-6989

Gloria Sings the Blues 3-2-74

Gloria feels depressed when she fears she might have fallen out of love with Michael.

Episode notes

- this is the episode that features the classic sock and a shoe exchange between Archie and Mike.

Pay the Twenty Dollars 3-9-74

Archie mistakenly gives George Jefferson a counterfeit $20 bill which causes a huge fight between them as well as Edith and Louise.

Episode notes
- Sherman Hemsley returns as George Jefferson.
- Isabel Sanford makes another appearance as Louise Jefferson.

Mike's Graduation 3-16-74

While Mike prepares for his final exams which will provide the opportunity for he and Gloria to move out, Archie makes plans to turn the kid's bedroom into a den.

Episode notes
- Betty Garrett makes an appearance as Irene Lorenzo.

SEASON FIVE

It is not uncommon for episodes of a television series not to air in the same order in which they were produced. Sometimes this is done out of necessity to accommodate schedules but in the case of All in the Family it was because its star had walked off the show, a threat which was being made with greater frequency as the series went on. While disagreements over creative direction were not uncommon for Carroll O'Conner, the actor now felt he was not being treated fairly and situations came to a boiling point. "I had to fight all the way and very often get nasty. I fault myself; I didn't have to get that nasty....they all used to put up a united front...yelling at me that the money wasn't there which of course is an enormous joke because ten times that money was there."[39] He further explained to the Associated Press "Salary was not in question...I wanted different working conditions. I wanted a Monday through Friday schedule and 12 shows off a year."[40] With the weight of the number one show in the country on his shoulders and a network that was billing record numbers in advertising, O'Connor walked away threatening that he would not return unless his concerns were acknowledged. Rob Reiner recalled "It was a struggle but it was a struggle from a standpoint of people wanting it to be better. The hardest kind of theater to do is when you mix social issues, drama, and comedy in a realistic and honest way and be entertaining. It's very hard to do but if you can pull it off it's the best theater there is."[41]

To cover these behind the scenes struggles, a multi-episode story was conceived where Archie takes a trip to reunite with his Army buddies but somehow gets lost as the family fears the worst. As a result, the episodes **Where's Archie**, **Archie Is Missing,** and **The Longest Kiss** are weak although the rest of the cast tries their best to make the material work. The episodes feel like filler but Norman Lear was not messing around and fully intended to kill off the Archie Bunker character if he and his temperamental star could not come to terms. By the time the third and final episode of the story arc aired, the behind-the-scenes drama was resolved and as Archie walked in to the Bunkers house in its closing moments, all was right with the world again at 704 Hauser Street... for the time being. The timing for this negotiation could not have been better and although O'Connor would not get his 12 episodes off a year (roughly half a season), he would get a nice pay hike. "If a show is number one, earning many, many millions of dollars....the network coughs up the extra loot. And I do mean cough! The hacking in New York can be heard live and unamplified in Hollywood. But be sure of this: if the demand is met, it is well within the limits of good business sense"[42] said O'Connor in 1979. Further changes and shakeups both in front of and behind the camera continued to change the structure of the hit show but at this moment, All in the Family was at the top of the ratings and enjoying enormous clout in the industry for such demands of its star to be fulfilled.

Roughly at the halfway point of the series (the 100th episode would air in December 1974 with a one-hour retrospective hosted by Henry Fonda), the tone of the series continued to evolve this season and look inward at the characters for sources of story material.

Feeling the pressure of the Watergate scandal, the Nixon era came to a grinding halt in August of 1974 when the President resigned and Vice President Gerald Ford took office. With Nixon's resignation went much of the angst that defined America in the early 1970s counterculture movement. The tone of the series began to reflect that change in attitude as the country began to heal. This is evident in the way that the character of Mike Stivic is portrayed this season. Now in a Graduate program at school and pursuing his masters, his appearance is slightly cleaned up with shorter hair and he can be seen wearing slacks more often than jeans. He is still very much in love with his wife yet the physical intensity between them has died down somewhat. His approach to things while no less passionate, is not filled with as much societal anger as he moves away from the safety of the classroom and closer to the working world that Archie inhabits.

While there are still plenty of opportunities for Archie to express his bigotry, those edges begin to soften. The character of Archie Bunker was successful because it was not a one joke performance. He was given dimensions and therefore allowed to grow. Archie was frustrated and insecure with the world around him. The things he said were many times unforgivable yet they were understandable because of the world in which he was raised.

Archie's faith in what his country stands for is shaken up a bit in the season premiere episode **The Bunkers and Inflation**. Played out over a four-episode story arc, it is a unique approach in that the multi-episode format allows time to richly explore the storyline and the effects of the economy on the Bunker household. The story starts with the Bunker's celebrating their 26th wedding anniversary and while preparations are being made, there are talks that Archie's Union will go on strike. Archie has finally purchased an engagement ring for Edith, something he was unable to do when he first asked her to marry him. When his Union strikes, it puts Archie out of work for several weeks. As time drags on with no resolution in site Archie's biggest fears are realized when Edith is offered a job - as cashier at George Jeffersons cleaning store! Archie objects but as negotiations drag out to the point where the Bunkers might have to apply for welfare, he surrenders his pride and allows Edith to take the job. Not only has Archie evolved a little by sending his wife to work but in doing so accepts the ultimate (for him) indignation by taking help from a black man; something his prejudice would not have allowed in previous seasons. The strike is eventually resolved and Archie defends his country as not giving up on him. Yet because of inflation and without the cost-of-living increase clause in their new contract, Archie will financially be behind the eight ball again within a year.

With episodes like this, the show continued to reflect real life struggles and lifestyles as Sally Struthers recalled "We weren't Make Room for Daddy and Father Knows Best. We weren't this perfect family that came to the table, everybody dressed in their Sunday best with perfect manners. People belched, toilets flushed, and there were arguments. Our clothes were lower middle class and our house was not particularly that clean and pretty and the furniture had a rip here and a snag there. I was very comfortable with that because I didn't grow up in a house in Portland Oregon where everything and everyone was perfect and I enjoyed being a member of a family on tv that would allow people watching to feel better about themselves and their family. I knew people would relate more to our family whether or not anyone in the family ever espoused any bigotry than would ever relate before to a family on tv."[43]

In **Lionel the Live-In**, Lionel and George continue to fight over Lionel's interracial future in-laws. The argument spills over into the Bunker's living room in the middle of the night and it is agreed that Lionel will stay with them until the problem can be resolved. Archie has yet another mouth to feed under his roof and tries to convince Lionel to go back to his own home by comparing his situation to the plot of the 1927 film The Jazz Singer. While their relationship has changed since their discussion in the season three-episode **Lionel Steps Out**, this exchange between Archie and Lionel is reminiscent of their early moments together. It will be the last time in the series that the two of them will sit down and have such a discussion.

The Jeffersons have several set pieces during the first half of the season and became such popular characters that a spin-off was imminent. On January 11, 1975 in another backdoor pilot titled **The Jeffersons Move on Up**, Edith says goodbye to Louise as she and George prepare to move to that deluxe apartment in the sky. The following week, The Jeffersons premiered with their own show and would go on for a successful eleven season run. Archie has lost his nemesis; a blue-collar man much like himself who took a windfall from a car accident settlement and is building a better life for his family, something Archie has yet been able to do. While Archie usually winds up worse off than where he started, the African-American is not only here to stay in Archie's life, he is doing better. Without the Jeffersons to play off of, Archie and the series would never be the same.

Without conferring with Gloria first, Mike announces to everyone that they are not going to have any children in **Gloria's Shock**. Gloria is adamant that she carries her own child however in seeking support from Edith, as she has on many occasions, their discussion has the reverse effect on Gloria this time and she changes her mind. When Edith tells Gloria that the main thing women were meant to do was to give birth, the liberated Gloria has a change of heart. She does not want her life to be defined by being a mother but instead a person who is useful, then maybe a mother. Mike invites his college buddy Stuart over in **Mike's Friend**. Gloria wants to be included in the evening and suggests playing charades. Mike dismisses her as he would rather sit and intellectualize with his friend. This triggers fear and resentment in Gloria. Fear that because of his experiences, Mike will one day outgrow her and resentment, not unlike Archie, that she is working to help support her husband. It is Stuart who makes Mike realize that things do not always have to be so serious and intense. Mike is put in his place and apologizes, acknowledging that she has supported him and he will gladly return the favor and support her through school once he gets a job. These resolutions and promises will not matter much at the beginning of the sixth season when Gloria announces she is pregnant. They will however remain a sticking point in their relationship when, after the kids move to California in season nine, her fears come to be realized and Mike has indeed somewhat outgrown her and Gloria makes a decision that puts their marriage in jeopardy.

Edith's cousin Amelia returns for a visit in **Amelia's Divorce**. On the surface, Amelia and her husband Russ are the ideal couple; Russ fawns over his wife with compliments and gestures. When Russ leaves with Archie to go to Kelcy's so the women can have some time together, he admits to Archie that he is chasing younger women and suggests that he has had several affairs. Back home Amelia confides in Edith that she feels Russ pulling away and confesses that of all the marriages in the family it is Edith and Archie's that is the most successful. After Archie and Russ return, Russ says they must leave so he can get back to work. Archie and Edith say nothing to each other of their respective talks that afternoon and they sit in silence as Archie reaches over to hold Edith's hand. They may not have the money and Archie may not compliment Edith enough but they have their love for each other.

Several episodes have more in common with standard sitcom plots than what All in the Family was known for. A life expectancy quiz in a magazine worries Archie when it says he will only live to the age of 57 in **Archie and the Quiz**. In **No Smoking**, Mike and Archie make a bet that Mike can go without eating for 48 hours and Archie can go without smoking. While very entertaining and well written, these episodes could easily be plots of any other sitcom. These types of shows would appear with greater frequency in subsequent seasons.

The Bunkers have paid the house off in **The Very Moving Day** and that is not the only reason to celebrate. Mike is graduating and he and Gloria have begun looking for a place to live. Finding rent in the area too high, their only option, much to Mike's dismay, is to rent George Jeffersons house next door. With Mike and Gloria moving out, the dynamic of the show would change when it returned the following fall.

There would be more changes behind the scenes. With the departure of John Rich at the end of season four, the entire 24 episode run of season five was directed by H. Wesley Kenney whose career dated back to the earliest days of television, producing, and directing for the DuMont Network. He would leave the director's chair at the end of this season. Don Nicholl, Michael Ross, and Bernie West who were integral in setting the tone and humor of the series in its first five years, left to form their own company NRW. They would go on to adapt yet another British sitcom Man About the House for US Television. When Three's Company premiered in March of 1977, it would be criticized for its exploitive and suggestive content just as All in the Family was received by some critics in 1971.

Three's Company was a huge hit with television viewers placing in the top ten for six of its eight seasons.

While nominated again for Outstanding Comedy Series with Carroll O'Connor, Jean Stapleton, and Rob Reiner all receiving nominations, All in the Family went home empty handed when the Emmy Awards were handed out that year. O'Connor and Stapleton were both nominated for along with the series for Best TV Show at the Golden Globes however Betty Garrett took home the sole award as Best Supporting Actress.

season five episodes

The Bunkers and Inflation 9-14-74
The Bunkers and Inflation-Archie Underfoot 9-21-74
The Bunkers and Inflation-
Edith the Job Hunter 9-28-74
The Bunkers and Inflation-Archie's Raise 10-5-74
With Archie's Union on strike, the family struggles to make ends meet with Gloria, Edith, and even Mike pitching in to lend financial assistance.

Episode notes
- Sherman Hemsley and Isabel Sanford appear as the Jeffersons across this story arc.
- Billy Halop appears in the first part as Munson.
- Betty Garrett appears in this story as Irene.

- Mike Evans co-stars as Lionel Jefferson.
- The Bunkers are celebrating their 26th anniversary as this story begins.
- In order to keep the party moving, Archie suggests that Irene play "We're in the Money" on her ukulele then immediately asks her to stop. This was the song he sang in the season four-episode **Archie the Gambler** which made Edith realize that he was gambling again. Given the circumstances in this episode, Archie does not feel the song is appropriate.
- In the first episode of this story, Mike and Archie conclude their argument about Nixon when it is mentioned that he had to resign his office as he knew about the cover-up.
- We first hear about President Ford in the fourth part of this story.
- In part two, Archie wants to watch the ballgame but the TV is on the fritz. He must not have purchased an extended warranty when he got a brand-new TV in the season three episode The Locket.
- This is the first appearance of James Cromwell as Stretch Cunningham in part four of the story. He would go on to star in the short-lived Norman Lear produced sitcom Hot L Baltimore which also featured All in the Family alums Richard Masur, Jeannie Linero, and Charlotte Rae. Cromwell carved a nice niche' for himself as a character actor in films

like L.A. Confidential (1997) and Babe (1995) for which he received an academy award nomination. Current TV viewers may also recognize him from Six Feet Under and Succession.

Lionel the Live-In 10-12-74

After a fight with his father about his fiancé Jenny, Lionel comes to stay with the Bunkers.

Episode notes

- Archie mentions that Lionel can stay in the attic, where cousin Oscar died in season two.
- Mike Evans returns as Lionel Jefferson.
- Sherman Hemsley co-stars as George Jefferson.
- Isabel Sanford makes an appearance as Louise Jefferson.

Archie's Helping Hand 10-19-74

Archie unknowingly helps Irene get a job as a forklift driver on the same dock where he works.

Episode notes

- Betty Garrett returns as Irene Lorenzo.
- With Vincent Gardenia long gone from the show as Frank Lorenzo, he is only mentioned in this episode as being gone a lot from home, which is why Irene is looking for something more to do.
- A reference is made to Edith getting a job to help out in the inflation story arc at the beginning of the season.

- It is revealed after Irene is hired that she makes as much as Archie - $5.50 an hour.
- Sorrell Brooke plays the part of Mr. Sanders the personnel manager. He was previously seen as the station manager in the season two-episode **Archie and the Editorial** and will return as Mr. Sanders in future episodes.

Gloria's Shock 10-26-74

Gloria is surprised to learn that Mike does not want to have children.

Episode notes
- Betty Garret co-stars as Irene Lorenzo.
- We have heard about the Jeffersons dog in the season three-episode Gloria the Victim. Here we learn that the Jeffersons also have a cat. However, when they move later in the season, neither animal is mentioned.

Where's Archie? (part I) 11-2-74
Where's Archie? – Archie is Missing (part II) 11-9-74
Where's Archie? – The Longest Kiss (part III) 11-16-74

When Archie fails to show up for an army reunion, the family worries that something bad may have happened to him.

Episode notes

- Carroll O'Connor does not appear in the first two parts of this story.
- Betty Garret makes an appearance in this story arc as Irene Lorenzo.
- Isabel Sanford returns as Louise Jefferson in this story.
- Sherman Hemsley appears as George Jefferson in this story.
- James Cromwell returns as Stretch Cunningham.
- Gloria LeRoy makes her first appearance in part two of this story as Mildred "Boom Boom" Turner and will reprise the role two more times. She previously guested as Bobbie Jo Loomis in the season three episode **The Threat**.
- Edith again mentions she has a younger brother.
- Charlotte Rae makes an appearance in the first part of this story. Rae had a long career going back to the early days of television in the classic sitcom Car 54 Where Are You?. She would find great fame and recognition later in the decade as housekeeper Mrs. Garrett on Diff'rent Strokes (1978-1985), a role which would spin off on to the successful sitcom The Facts of Life (1979-1988)
- In part one, the Estrada's – the new neighbors from season four –attend Edith's Tupperware party only they are played by different performers.

- Mike and Gloria attempt to attend a Marx Brothers film festival during the first part of this story arc. A Marx Brothers revival was in full swing at this time due to the re-release of their 1930 classic Animal Crackers earlier in the summer of 1974. The film had been out of circulation for the last few decades due to copyright issues with the authors of the original stage play. Animal Crackers would make its television debut on CBS on July 21st, 1979.

Archie and the Miracle 11-23-74

Archie dedicates himself to helping at the church after a near fatal accident at work.

Episode notes
- Betty Garrett returns as Irene Lorenzo.
- James Cromwell makes his final appearance as Stretch Cunningham.
- Archie enters the church raffle for a brand-new color TV. Apparently, the new TV he purchased in season three was a lemon seeing as it already broke down earlier in the season.
- Archie says that his lucky number is 18. It is the day his life was saved, his birthday, his locker number at work, and the day he met Edith (although she has to remind him of that one).

George and Archie Make a Deal 11-30-74

George Jefferson enters politics and wants Archie to sign a petition for his support so he can break through a wall and expand his cleaning store. In exchange, Archie negotiates a break on the cleaning for the family.

Episode notes

- A reference is made in this episode about the petition Archie was passing around to keep minorities out of the neighborhood in the season four opener **We're Having a Heat Wave**.
- Sherman Hemsley and Isabel Sanford appear as the Jeffersons.
- We find out in this episode that Archie's signature is not any good as he still is not registered to vote.

Archie's Contract 12-7-74

Archie makes a deal with a shady salesman to put aluminum siding on his house.

Episode notes

- Betty Garrett appears as Irene Lorenzo in this episode.
- The part of the policeman is played by Ed Peck. He previously appeared on the series in the season three-episode **Archie's Fraud** and would have a recurring role on Happy Days as Officer Kirk.

- The part of Mr. Scanlon is played by Dennis Patrick. He will return in season eight as Gordie Lloyd. Patrick had almost 175 appearances to his credit including the Six Million Dollar Man, Dallas, and It's Garry Shandling's Show.
- Mike says that the Bunker's house is made of brick yet whenever we see the exterior of the front of the house it is not.

Mike's Friend 12-14-74
Mike invites his friend Stuart over and shuts Gloria out in the process of their visit together.

Episode notes
- Stuart is played by Greg Mullavey who would go on to star in the Norman Lear produced Mary Hartman, Mary Hartman.
- Carroll O'Connor does not appear in this episode as he was still in a contract dispute with producer Norman Lear.

The Best of All in the Family (one hour) 12-21-74
Henry Fonda hosts a retrospective featuring clips from the first five seasons of the show.

Prisoner in the House 1-4-75

Archie is uncomfortable when he finds out that the plumber's helper is really on a work furlough plan from jail.

Episode notes

- This episode recalls the fourth season episode **Gloria's Boyfriend** in that an outsider again connects with the Bunkers.
- Cliff Osmond plays Nick the plumber's helper. He can also be seen in many other shows of the 60s and 70s including Batman, Mod Squad, and Six Million Dollar Man.

The Jeffersons Move on Up 1-11-75

The Jeffersons move out of Queens to their own apartment in Manhattan. This served as the pilot for the Jeffersons.

Episode notes

- Jean Stapleton is the only All in the Family cast member to appear in this episode.
- The parts of Tom and Helen Willis are recast with Franklin Cover and Roxie Roker.
- The part of Lionel's fiancé Jenny is also recast with Berlinda Tolbert.

All's Fair 1-18-75

After reading a book on fair fighting, Mike and Gloria try to convince Edith that there is a better approach to arguing with Archie.

Amelia's Divorce 1-25-75

During a visit by her cousin Amelia, Edith learns that Amelia wants a divorce.

Episode notes
- Rob Reiner and Sally Struthers do not appear in this episode.
- Bob Hastings appears as Kelsey.
- The parts of Amelia and Russ are played this time by Elizabeth Wilson and George S. Irving.

Everybody Does It 2-8-75

Archie tries to justify taking a box of nails from work, which initiates a discussion about how everyone cheats to a certain extent.

Episode notes
- Betty Garret returns as Irene Lorenzo.

Archie and the Quiz 2-15-75

Archie is worried about his life expectancy when a magazine quiz kills him off at 57.

Episode notes

- When Edith makes the calculations, she betters Archie's life by 6.4 years while she herself will live to 84 years and 6 months. Edith will eventually pass away before Archie.
- Archie says that his dad died at age 57, yet Archie turned 50 in the season four-episode **Archie Feels Left Out**. The math does not add up as in the series premiere **Meet the Bunkers**, both of his parents are still alive; having paid him a visit the year before.

Edith's Friend 2-22-75

While attending a wedding that Archie did not want to go to, Edith reconnects with a childhood sweetheart.

Episode notes

- The dress Edith mentions wearing for her 26th anniversary is different than the dress she wore in that episode (**The Bunkers and Inflation part 1**).
- The part of Roy Johnson is played by Tim O'Connor who had over 100 credits to his name including Peyton Place, The Streets of San Francisco, and Buck Rogers in the 25th Century. He died on April 5, 2018

No Smoking 3-1-75

Mike and Archie make a bet that Mike can fast for 48 hours and Archie cannot smoke.

Episode notes

- In an attempt to show Archie, it will be healthy to stop smoking for 48 hours, Gloria mentions the quiz results from that previous episode.
- When Mike and Archie get in bed together, Mike is reading All the President's Men, the book about the Watergate cover-up.

Mike Makes His Move 3-8-75

As the Bunker's celebrate paying off the house, Mike makes plans for he and Gloria to move out.

Episode notes

- The Bunkers had a 20-year mortgage and with it now paid off, this will give Archie the bargaining power he needs to purchase Kelsey's Bar in season eight.
- Betty Garrett appears as Irene Lorenzo.
- Burt Mustin returns as Mr. Quigley.
- Ruth McDevitt makes her final appearance as Jo Nelson.
- Billy Halop appears again as Munson.
- Sherman Hemsley makes another appearance as George Jefferson.

- Mike Evans makes his final appearance of the series as Lionel Jefferson.
- Bob Hastings makes another appearance as Kelsey.
- As Mike leaves the house to look for an apartment he exclaims "You won't have Mike Stivic to kick around anymore!" and makes two peace signs with his hands in reference to Richard Nixon's "last press conference" in 1962.
- Mr. Jefferson channels his inner Godfather when he tells Lionel that he is going to make Mike an "offer he can't refuse."

Television changed in the years since All in the Family premiered. After occupying the lead in spot for the CBS Saturday night lineup in its previous four seasons, All in the Family moved to Monday nights at 9pm Eastern for its sixth year however this was not by choice. The days of Lucy and The Brady Bunch were over and with the increase in socially aware sitcoms and gritty, violent dramas – for their time - like Kojak and The Streets of San Francisco, some viewers and critics began to complain that the changing landscape of television could have a negative reaction on its viewers and possibly society as a whole. With mounting pressure from the Federal Communications Commission (FCC), the National Association of Broadcasters (NAB) created the family viewing hour. This meant that no show of a controversial nature could be aired between 8 to 9pm Eastern Time.

Not only did All in the Family move timeslots, it moved studios. Taped at Television City for its first five seasons, production moved to the newly constructed Metromedia Square early in season six for the remainder of its run. With Norman Lear supervising so many shows (including

All in the Family, Maude, Good Times, The Jeffersons, and the newly created One Day at a Time which would launch in December of 1975), it logistically made sense for him to move all production under one roof.

It was around this time as well that Fred Silverman, who was responsible for bringing All in the Family to television, jumped ship to ABC and began positioning their lineup to help boost the visibility of the network. Within time as the socially based sitcoms began to run their course and adapt to a yet again changing culture, it was ABC with family friendly shows like Happy Days (a show Silverman tried to kill and counterprogram with Good Times the previous season) and Laverne and Shirley which would start to dominate the ratings. Silverman would also be instrumental in giving the go ahead for Three's Company, a series created by All in the Family alumni Don Nicholl, Michael Ross, and Bernie West.

Prior to production of the sixth season, Sally Struthers asked to be released from her contract so she could pursue a feature film career and as a result does not appear in two episodes (**Archie the Hero** and **Chain Letter**). An unsuccessful breach of contract lawsuit followed which resulted in the star being quite unpleasant around her castmates. A blow-up between Struthers and Carroll O'Conner ensued which reportedly left Struthers in tears but recentered her and she returned to work.

Regardless of the talent behind the scenes, a six-year-old show does start to show its age. All in the Family was no different. Even with a shakeup in the format, the series still had a strong voice and there was much left to say. The show maintained a strong connection with the viewing audience as the sixth season began in the Fall of 1975. Viewers followed the Bunkers to Monday night and kept the show at the top of the ratings. This watershed season for the series is uneven and would be its last as the number one show in America.

With much of the original creative team behind the scenes having departed, it is no surprise that the change in staff presented a different approach to the series. Lou Derman had been a story editor on the show since season five. He would serve as producer, script supervisor, and pen ten episodes this season. Derman also wrote for one of television's earliest sitcoms December Bride and was a writer on Here's Lucy, Lucille Ball's third go around on the small screen. Hal Kanter, whose resume included writing credits with Martin and Lewis, Bob Hope, and Milton Berle, was executive producer for six episodes and contributed to two scripts. He also created the landmark series Julia for which he wrote several episodes. Larry Rhine wrote for Bob Hope and Red Skelton and would provide the teleplays and scripts for over 30 episodes in the final four seasons. Mel Tolken was a writer on Your Show of Shows, I'm Dickens, He's Fenster, and The

Danny Kaye Show. He would write thirty stories through the end of the series. Bill Davenport wrote six episodes in the fifth season and would go on to write another seven in this season. His credits include some of the staples of early television such as The Fibber McGee and Molly Show, Make Room For Daddy, and December Bride. Milt Josefsberg came on board with a resume which included work for Jack Benny and Lucille Ball. He would start out as the story editor and eventually be promoted to producer and script supervisor for the remainder of the series. Paul Bogart primarily dabbled in television drama such as The Defenders and Kraft Theatre occasionally stepping away from the genre to direct comedies like Get Smart. He had several television movies and feature films to his credit including Bob Hope's final starring cinematic outing, 1972s Cancel My Reservation and Dean Martin's final starring film Mr. Ricco (1975). Bogart would take the director's chair this season and would remain the director for the last four seasons of the show. His background in drama would help tremendously with navigating the cast through some of the more dramatic moments of the series final years.

With so much of the behind-the-scenes talent rooted in classic comedy involving many of its pioneers, it impacts how Archie is presented for the remainder of the series. While speaking in malapropisms was always a part of his speech pattern, they start to appear with greater frequency this season. It's as if he cannot get a single sentence out without mangling a word along the way. There was always an articulateness in his lack of articulacy. Whatever intelligence the character possessed; it starts to fade away beginning with this season. In several scenes he is played as a bumbler who has more in common with the slapstick era of comedy, including exaggerated facial expressions and pantomime, than the Archie Bunker we have come to know up to this point. While there are still scenes and episodes where we are reminded of Archie's roots, a tender side also starts to emerge in the character which is a welcome change when we consider some of the challenges Archie and Edith will face throughout the end of the series. Yet, overall, Archie becomes more buffoonish starting with this season.

Mike, now a professor, takes on a more conservative look and more than half of this season's output deal with stories which revolve around Gloria's pregnancy, the birth of the baby, or Mike and Gloria adjusting as independent adults and new parents no longer under Archie's roof. The Ideal Toy Company jumped on the bandwagon, manufacturing an Archie Bunker's Grandson Joey Stivic "drink & wet" doll. In several episodes such as **Mike's Pains, Gloria Is Nervous, Mike's Move, New Year's Wedding**, and **Love by Appointment**, all the action takes place in the Stivics' home and all play like a potential spin-off series. The problems of the post 704 Hauser Street Mike and Gloria are not as interesting and are even less entertaining than in previous seasons. It is not an insult to the actors playing the roles, as Reiner and Struthers do the best they can. Perhaps it is the background of the writing team that does not appear to connect with the modern-day experiences of Mike and Gloria which results in some mediocre material. Other episodes focus solely on Archie and Edith with the kids merely walking in and out of scenes to remind us they are still a part of the show. These story lines play much better as do the stories where all four characters have consistent interaction throughout the episode. It shows how important the dynamic was when they were all under one roof together. When that dynamic changed, so did the show.

With Gloria announcing she is pregnant at the beginning of the season in **The Very Moving Day**, Mike is initially ecstatic about the arrival of their child. When Gloria reminds him of all the concerns he has so strongly voiced against bringing a child into the world (most recently in the season five-episode **Gloria's Shock**), his joy turns to panic as he storms out of the house after telling Gloria she tricked him by getting pregnant. Alone, Gloria finds solace in Archie who holds her in his arms in his favorite chair and recounts the story of when he first saw her as a baby. Like the season one episode **Gloria is Pregnant**, there is a poignancy in this moment where the love between a father and his daughter is very genuine which Stuthers related in a 2021 article with Closer Weekly "In 1968, my own father passed away. I was still feeling bad and fatherless when I got this show. Carroll and his wife, Nancy, turned out to be as parental with me as he was in the show. Carroll gave me advice, he laughed at my antics, he hugged me all the time"[44] Mike looks to Irene Lorenzo for comfort and she reminds him that for someone so liberal, he could always have gotten a vasectomy if he felt so strongly about not having children. She produces a poem that she has saved which calms Mike's fears and puts the happy news back into perspective for him. Bringing a child into a show can always be looked at as a gimmick to help boost ratings however at the time, the series did not need such help and given the change in logistics, it seemed like the natural progression for the characters. It is interesting to note that Gloria accepts this change in direction after having a much different resolution to the topic in previous episodes, most recently season five's **Mike's Friend**.

Attempting to score points for a dispatcher promotion, Archie unknowingly signs an organ donor card in **Archie the Doner**. When he backs out telling the personnel manager it is because his insides are not good according to his doctor, he gets passed over for the promotion and Elmo Bridgewater (Black Elmo) is promoted to dispatcher.

In **Grandpa Blues** there may be a layoff at Archie's company and either Archie or "old man" Dirksmeier are going to be let go. Archie goes for an initial physical where he is told that he must reduce his blood pressure. Upon hearing that Mike and Gloria may name their new child Stanislaus, he gets so irritated that Edith throws the kids out of the house so Archie can rest. She innocently asks Archie if he would like to go upstairs which Archie of course interprets otherwise. Edith embarrassingly smiles at Archie and he takes her by the hand to lead her upstairs. While there have been suggestions that the Bunkers have been intimate in previous seasons, this is the only overt example thus far and it is such a charming scene. The studio audience agreed and responded with warm laughter and applause.

Mike has been tutoring Linda Galloway in **Gloria Suspects Mike** and Gloria fears Mike is cheating on her. Archie decides he is going to get the truth out of Mike by getting him drunk. The scene where Mike and Archie are drunk together is priceless as Archie toasts the greatest country in the world – Poland. Archie tells Mike that the Meathead days are over. He will call him Michael from now on and asks that Michael call him Dad(dy). A drunk Mike in turn gives Archie a kiss on the forehead and puts him to bed on the couch after he's passed out. Mike sings "Oh My Papa" as he stumbles out of the house. While the scenes of Archie and Mike drunk play as the stereotypical slurring and stumbling sitcom drunk, they are played to perfection and the comic timing between the two actors is hilarious.

In the Thanksgiving themed episode **The Little Atheist** Archie argues that baby Joey should be baptized and go to church but Mike and Gloria do not want their child to be able to make that choice. Archie loves his grandson and when he left to take care of him in **Archie the Babysitter**, we are shown just what a loving and caring man he is and what a father he must have been when Gloria was a baby.

Baby Joey finally arrives in a two-part story **Birth of the Baby** which is presented to viewers for the Christmastime episode of season six. The anxiety of Gloria being due at any minute is clumsily played against Archie trying to back out of doing a minstrel show for his lodge. Fearing his lodge brothers will kick him out, he goes ahead with the performance. Gloria goes into labor while her and Mike are at dinner and everyone meets up at the hospital including Archie who is still in his blackface. They all (including the nurse) start laughing at Archie's appearance. Even Mike, who earlier in the story denounced Archie and his friends for doing such a thing, breaks down into uncontrollable laughter. The scene comes off clumsy and silly rather than funny and has more in common with an episode of I Love Lucy in its approach than an episode of All in the Family. Given the combined resume of the majority of the new production staff, this comes as no surprise.

In **Joey's Baptism**, Archie sneaks Joey away to be baptized although Mike is dead set against it. When the Reverend Chung tells Archie he cannot perform the ceremony without the parents' permission, Archie takes matters into his own hands and baptizes Joey himself telling the Lord "They're gonna kill me when I get home." In somewhat of a continuation of the story, Archie and Edith spend the night as **Mike and Gloria's Houseguests** when the Bunker's furnace breaks down. Mike, still upset from the baptism, initially does not want Archie in his home so Archie decides to sleep in the Bunkers' kitchen. With one mishap after another (he knocks a box of cereal over, breaks a shelf, and breaks a window) Archie reluctantly goes next door where the argument continues until a power outage makes them forget what they were fighting about. This episode is somewhat of a reworking of another episode from earlier in the season titled **Alone at Last.** After declaring his independence from Archie and storming out of the house, Mike forgets to call and have the utilities turned on in his new home so he and Gloria commit to staying in their cold new home. Edith also leaves Archie to be with the kids because he will not apologize for his behavior. In yet another kitchen scene, Archie burns a steak, knocks over another bowl of cereal, knocks over a bottle of dressing, and basically fumbles his way around the kitchen. While very entertaining with each mishap timed perfectly, it is the type of scene that would feel more at home in a Laurel and Hardy short subject than an episode of the series.

Edith exerts herself more in two very entertaining episodes which showcase the talents and range of Jean Stapleton. With Gloria out of the house and Irene Lorenzo taking less of an active role in Edith's life, **Edith Steps Out** and starts volunteering her time at the Sunshine Home for the elderly. Archie is threatened at the prospect of losing attention from Edith especially when it's for "nothing" work that she is not being paid for which hurts her feelings. A guilty Archie takes Edith to dinner where she informs him that she no longer is a volunteer. The Sunshine Home loves her work so much they have decided to hire her! In **Edith's Night Out**, Archie shows no interest in going out and spending time with Edith so she goes down to Kelcy's for a change to get away from Archie. There, she is the life of the party and when Archie arrives, not knowing she has gone down there, he is threatened once again by her independence. He tells her that he will take her out for dinner and a Knicks game the following weekend if she will just go home with him. Edith all but cinches the offer by telling everyone in the bar of Archie's plans and if he backs out, she will be back for a visit the following weekend. Edith has always had Archie's number as far back as the season one episode **Gloria Discovers Women's Lib** and knew how to handle him without injuring his fragile ego but as with many dutiful wives across sitcom history, Archie was never the wiser. Her experiences and friendships with women like Louise Jefferson and Irene Lorenzo over the ensuing seasons imbued the character with a confidence and attractiveness to not only get her way but make sure Archie is aware that she is getting her way. This change in character direction will continue to soften Archie in subsequent seasons.

In one of the more memorable episodes of the season, Archie saves the life of a woman in his cab in **Archie the Hero** only he comes to find out that she was man dressed as a woman. Born Don Seymour McLean, Lori Shannon was a real-life female impersonator. The scene where she reveals herself as a man to Archie is hysterical and she would make two very memorable appearances over the next two seasons.

The standout episode of the season is **Archie Finds a Friend**. In this one, Archie befriends a poor and lonely Jewish watchmaker named Mr. Bernstein. Bernstein has an invention, a remote doorbell ringer, and has approached Archie as an investor. The invention needs to be adjusted because it rings every doorbell in the neighborhood. While on the surface another get rich quick scheme, there is a sincerity this time around. By his own admission Archie does not have the brains to come up with such an invention but for the first time, someone outside of his family genuinely needs him. Although Archie does not even know the man's first name, these two souls find a usefulness together because they can relate to one another; working class guys trying to make each of their lives a little better. They play odds or evens and Mr. Bernstein always wins because Archie always puts up the same number of fingers. With the excitement of his dream becoming a reality, Mr. Bernstein collapses. Calling for his doctor, Edith discovers he has a bad heart. As she comforts him, the dying man tells her "Mrs. Bunker, for you I'd like to make the bells ring all over the world like Christmas Eve." You understand in this moment what a valuable contribution she must make to the Sunshine Home. One more game of odds or evens but this time Bernstein lets Archie win and passes away. Archie and Edith go out on the porch where Archie presses the remote doorbell ringer so all the bells in the neighborhood can ring out to simulate a respectful funeral dirge.

The series was nominated again for Outstanding Comedy Series at the Emmy's and Best Television Series however it would lose to The Mary Tyler Moore Show. Best Actor (for Carroll O'Connor), Best Supporting Actor (Rob Reiner), and Best Television Series nominations would be made at the Golden Globes for 1976 however the series would not receive any awards for this season.

season six episodes

The Very Moving Day 9-8-75
Gloria announces she is pregnant as her and Mike prepare to move out of the Bunkers' house

Episode notes
- Betty Garret appears as Irene Lorenzo.
- There is a new opening credit sequence for the series and now the actors' names appear before the name of the show (in part due to Carroll O'Connor's contract negotiation the previous year).

Alone at Last 9-75-75
The kids spend the first night in their home only Mike has forgotten to turn on the utilities.

Episode notes
- In the season one episode **Lionel Moves Into the Neighborhood**, Archie mentions the layout of the Jeffersons house is the same as his. Now that we finally get to see it, we can see that it is a completely different layout. Even the counter we have seen in the kitchen in previous episodes has vanished.
- Archie bets on a baseball game yet Edith makes no objections to it.

Archie the Doner 9-22-75

To try and get ahead for an upcoming dispatcher promotion, Archie unknowingly signs up for the organ donor program at work.

Episode notes

- Betty Garrett appears as Irene Lorenzo.
- While we have only heard about him up to now, we get to meet Black Elmo for the one and only time in this episode and learn his last name is Bridgewater. He is played by J.A. Preston who would go on to appear in Hill Street Blues and Dallas as well as numerous other tv series.

Archie the Hero 9-29-75

Archie saves the life of a woman in his cab only to find out that she is a transvestite.

Episode notes

- Sally Struthers does not appear in this episode.
- Beverly LaSalle is played by female impersonator Lori Shannon.
- Edith mentions that she stayed at the Northern Motor Inn (where Beverly is currently performing) when she was on jury duty back in season one.
- Billy Halop returns as Munson.
- Bob Hastings makes an appearance as Kelsey.

- Sandy Kenyon makes his second of three appearances on All in the Family in this episode playing the part of Jim Kitchener.

Mike's Pains 10-16-75

Mike struggles with wanting to be in the room with Gloria while she gives birth. Meanwhile Sybil Gooley gives Gloria the ring test to determine if her baby will be a boy or a girl (for the record – she said it would be a boy)

Episode notes

- This is the first time we are introduced to Sybil Gooley.

Chain Letter 10-20-75

After breaking a chain letter, Archie fears he may have contracted hepatitis from a chug-a-lug contest.

Episode notes

- Bob Hastings is back at the bar as Kelsey.
- Billy Halop appears as Munson.
- Betty Garrett makes an appearance as Irene Lorenzo.
- This is the first time the Bunker's physician Dr. Shapiro is mentioned.
- Sally Struthers does not appear in this episode.
- Robert Guillaume plays the part of the doctor. He is perhaps best known as Benson in both Soap

and its self-titled spinoff. He also appeared on the acclaimed series Sports Night.
- The nurse is played by Beatrice Colen who also appeared in The Odd Couple, Wonder Woman, and Happy Days.

Mike Faces Life 10-27-75

Mike's pacifist views are challenged when Gloria is unfairly fired from her job for being pregnant.

Episode notes
- The part of Gordon Crenshaw is played by George Furth. He was previously featured in the first season episode **Archie's Aching Back** and appeared in many classic television series and films including Butch Cassidy and the Sundance Kid (1969) and Blazing Saddles (1974)
- Although Gloria is hired back at the end of the episode, this is the last time we hear about her working at Kresslers.

Edith Breaks Out 11-3-75

Edith stands up to Archie when she begins volunteering at the Sunshine Home.

Episode notes
- This is the first episode where it is mentioned that Edith is volunteering
- When Edith is hired, she is paid $2 an hour.

- Sally Struthers does not appear in this episode.
- James Hong plays the waiter at Hop Sings. He was previously seen in the first season episode **Archie Gives Blood** and has over 400 film and television appearances to his credit.

Grandpa Blues 11-10-75

Archie must lower his blood pressure to pass a company physical to keep his job.

Episode notes
- Stanislaus is the first name of Mike's Dad.
- The part of the nurse is played by Tracy Bogart who is the daughter of series director Paul Bogart. This is the first of three appearances for her in the series.

Gloria Suspects Mike 11-17-75

Gloria fears that Mike is having an affair with a student he is tutoring.

Episode notes
- Broadway veteran Bernadette Peters appears as Linda Galloway in this episode. Peters made appearances on several television and variety shows in the 1970's. She would co-star with Richard Crenna the following for the one season sitcom All's Fair which was created by Norman Lear.

The Little Atheist 11-24-75

While celebrating Thanksgiving, Archie and Mike disagree if Mike will raise his son in the church and get him baptized.

Episode notes

- Betty Garrett makes an appearance as Irene Lorenzo.
- Gloria is eight months pregnant in this episode.

Archie's Civil Rights 12-1-75

Archie is brought to court over using pepper spray to scare away a mugger who was trying to rob him.

Episode notes

- Rob Reiner does not appear in this episode.
- Archie tells the judge that he met Sammy Davis Jr. in reference to that season two-episode.
- Frank Camppanella returns to the series in another authority role as the police officer. He previously played Detective Sgt. Perkins in the season two-episode **Archie Sees a Mugging**.
- Charles Siebert makes his first of three appearances on the show. He can also be seen in the season seven episode **Stretch Cunningham, Goodbye** and the season nine-episode **Edith's Final Respects**.

Gloria is Nervous 12-8-75

Nine weeks overdue, Gloria becomes nervous about having the baby.

- Carroll O'Connor does not appear in this episode.
- Betty Garrett makes her final appearance as Irene Lorenzo
- This was the first episode of the series taped at Metromedia Square.

Birth of the Baby (part I) 12-15-75
Birth of the Baby (part II) 12-22-75
Gloria gives birth to baby Joey.

Episode notes

- We get the first glimpse of the Bunker's bathroom in part one.
- While we have heard several times that Archie belongs to a lodge, we never learn the name of it until this episode – The Kings of Queens. The number to the lodge is 555-4378.
- Allan Melvin appears as Barney Hefner.
- Herb Voland plays fellow lodge brother Ed Bradley. Voland appeared in dozens of TV shows and may be best known as General Clayton on M*A*S*H.
- In part two of the story, Archie mentions Gloria being stuck in the phone booth only nobody has told him about that.

- During the restaurant scene, Mike and Gloria reminisce about their first date at the Mets game. Gloria asks him if he remembers what the band was playing and they both start singing the Star-Spangled Banner. Yet, in the season two-episode **Edith the Judge**, Mike denounces the song for glorifying war making no reference that it had a bit of sentimental meaning to him.
- Priscilla Morrill plays Bernice the nurse in this episode. She was featured as a nurse in the season three-episode **Archie in the Hospital** and one of Edith's classmates in that seasons **Class Reunion**.
- Barbara Cason plays Dorothy the nurse. She was previously on the series in the season two episode **The Election Story** and will return in season nine in **Edith Gets Fired**.

New Year's Wedding 1-5-76
Mike and Gloria host a wedding in their house for their friends Al and Trudy.

Episode notes
- Al is played by Bill Crystal who would go on to appear in his breakthrough role as Jody on Soap and continue a successful career on stage, television, and screen in such films as City Slickers (1991) and the 1989 comedy When Harry Met Sally (directed by Rob Reiner)

- Gloria's friend Trudy is played by Elaine Princi in this episode.
- Carroll O'Connor and Jean Stapleton do not appear in this episode.
- The quote that Gloria gives to Mike to read during the ceremony was read at her and Mike's wedding. Only no such quote was read in that season three-episode **Flashback: Mike and Gloria's Wedding**. The quote will appear again in the season eight finale **The Stivics Go West**.
- Joey is two weeks old in this episode.
- The part of Reverend Harris is played by Michael Mann. This is the first of three appearances for Mann on All in the Family. Mann will return the following season as Dr. Doby in **Gloria's False Alarm** and later in season nine as Rabbi Jacobs in **Stephanie's Conversion**. He can also be seen in such shows as Taxi, and Laverne and Shirley as well as the feature films Smokey and the Bandit (1977), Coma (1978), and The China Syndrome (1979)

Archie the Babysitter 1-12-76
Not trusting the girl that Mike and Gloria have hired to watch Joey, Archie takes the babysitting duties into his own hands.

Episode notes

- This was the last episode taped at Television City.
- Jean Stapleton does not appear in this episode.
- Bob Hastings appears as Kelsey in this episode.
- The role of Archie's poker buddy Tiny is played by Jack Somack. Somack appeared as Tony Vicino in the season two-episode **Archie Sees a Mugging**.

Archie Finds a Friend 1-26-76

Archie befriends a Jewish watch repairman who has an invention he wants Archie to invest in.

Episode notes

- Although Archie refers to having a brother in the season two-episode **The Saga of Cousin Oscar** and the season three-episode **Lionel Steps Out**, he says he is an only child in this episode.
- Archie mentions that the remote doorbell set off the doorbell at the Weidermeyer's only they moved out at the beginning of season four and their house was purchased by the Lorenzo's.
- We first see the Bunker's porch in this episode although in the opening credits, the house used for filming the exteriors does not have a porch.
- Television veteran Jack Gilford plays Mr. Bernstein. Gilford had numerous TV credits to his name including Get Smart, The Defenders, Police Woman,

and co-starred in the Norman Lear created Apple Pie which ran for one season in 1978.

Mike's Move 2-2-76

Up for a promotion to Minnesota, Mike faces reverse discrimination when he finds out the other candidate is black.

Episode notes

- The part of John Kasten is played by David Downing who guested on such shows as What's Happening, Little House on the Prairie, The Fresh Prince of Bel-Air, and The Bernie Mac Show.
- Dean Winslow is played by Lee Bergere who also had roles in such series' as Hogan's Heroes, Emergency!, and co-starred on the Norman Lear created Hot L Baltimore which ran for one season in 1975.

Archie's Weighty Problem 2-9-76

Archie's doctor wants him to lose weight so Edith puts him on a diet.

Episode notes

- Burt Mustin makes his final appearance as Mr. Justin Quigley. Mustin passed away January 28, 1977 at the age of 92.
- Bob Hastings makes his final appearance as Kelsey. Hastings died on June 30, 2014 at the age of 89.

- Billy Halop makes his final appearance as Munson. Halop passed away nine months to the day this episode aired at age 56.

Love By Appointment 2-16-76
After having the baby, Mike is finding it difficult to be intimate with Gloria.

Joey's Baptism 2-23-76
Archie sneaks Joey out to baptize him.

Episode notes
- Joey is supposedly four months old in this episode.
- Clyde Kusatsu makes his first of several appearances as the Reverend Chong. He has appeared in numerous shows ranging from M*A*S*H to more recently the Netflix series Avatar: The Last Airbender.

Mike and Gloria's Houseguests 3-1-76
With the furnace broken at the Bunker's house, Archie and Edith spend the night at Mike and Gloria's.

Episode notes
- To avoid staying at the kids' house, Archie suggests that he and Edith go stay at the Airport Inn and have their second honeymoon, only they had their second honeymoon already in the season four-episode **Second Honeymoon**.

- Archie estimates Mike owes him $3,840 for staying in his house for five years. Mike's figures are a little more conservative at $2,600
- Archie says that Mike owes him for his appendix operation yet in that season three-episode Archie says he will pick up the tab.
- This is the first episode to acknowledge Ronald Reagan being a part of the political arena.

Edith's Night Out 3-8-76

Fed up with Archie's disinterest in spending time with her, Edith leaves the house and goes to Kelcy's.

Episode notes

- In this episode we find out that Archie used to take Edith to the movies every Tuesday so they could register for the free dishes that the theatre would give away.
- This is the first of many appearances for Jason Wingreen as Harry Snowden, the bartender at Kelcy's. He will continue as a featured player when the show transitions to Archie Bunker's Place in 1979. In a film and television career that spanned almost 40 years, he appeared on everything from The Bravados (1958) to the usual TV fare such as The Untouchables, The Twilight Zone, The Green Hornet, Night Gallery, and a semi-recurring role as Judge Arthur Beaumont on Matlock. In 1980, he

would lend his voice talents yet receive no credit as the voice of Boba Fett in The Empire Strikes Back.

- Marge is played by Doris Roberts who is probably best known as Ray Romano's Mom on the hit series Everybody Loves Raymond.
- Scott Brady plays the part of Joe Foley and would reprise the role in the season seven premiere.

The seventh year of All in the Family is an improvement over the previous season. Most of the episodes this season rely on the group dynamic which the series lacked the previous year. Like The Mary Tyler Moore Show, M*A*S*H, and Seinfeld, what made All in the Family successful was that it was an ensemble show. Once that formula changed, the show started to lose something. While there are still episodes which focus on either of the couples, one does not feel such episodes dominate this season when viewed in its entirety. Season seven is more consistently pleasing with its material.

An even bigger change occurs with Archie in season seven. Archie 1976 has more in common with his television ancestors Ralph Kramden and Throckmorton P. Gildersleeve than he does with the Archie of 1971. Archie's facial expressions, mannerisms, and delivery are more akin to the droll delivery of W.C. Fields. He is stripped of his credentials even more this season and a softer side of his personality continues to emerge. His bigoted roots continue to drive some of the dialog yet they are toned down considerably. At this point in the series, those components of his personality were no longer necessary to drive storylines. Archie is more openly affectionate to Edith now and is more willing to show his vulnerability. He hugs her, kisses her, and verbally expresses his feelings for her. He no longer tells her to "stifle" quite as much he only calls her a dingbat twice throughout the course of the season. With all that seemingly working against the character viewers became used to, Carroll O'Connor displays some of his finest acting in such episodes as the season opener **Archie's Brief Encounter** and the 1976 Christmas offering **The Draft Dodger**. Edith continues to anchor Archie and displays a stronger, more independent side. Her work at the Sunshine Home broadens her horizons even further. Her growth as a character in the first six years of the show really has an impact when one views **Archie's Brief Encounter** and **Archie's Secret Passion**. The difference in this season above any of the others that preceded it is that Archie is now willing to listen to Edith instead of cutting her off and treating her like more of a subordinate. There is even a hint that Archie and Edith are intimate with one another more frequently than we have been led to believe up to this point.

The show moved yet again to Wednesday's at 9pm from its Monday 9:30pm timeslot where it was replaced by the single season Norman Lear developed sitcom All's Fair starring Richard Crenna, Bernadette Peters, and featuring Michael Keaton in one of his earliest television roles. All in the Family was now the lead-in for a freshman show Alice (based on the 1972 film Alice Doesn't Live Here Anymore). The loyal audience would not follow this time and All in the Family not only fell out of the number one spot in the ratings, it fell out of the top ten entirely.

The series would rank #12 for the season right behind Three's Company which, like All in the Family, was based on a UK sitcom (Man About the House) and adapted by former All in the Family writers Don Nicholl, Michael Ross, and Bernie West. Former CBS executive Fred Silverman, who was responsible for bringing All in the Family to television in 1971, was now over at ABC and had 7 shows in the top 10 including Laverne and Shirley, Charlie's Angels, and the number one show in the country Happy Days. Meanwhile, none of the other established Norman Lear sitcoms (The Jeffersons, Good Times, Maude) ranked in the top 20 for the season. Not only did Maude miss the top 20, it did not even rank in the top thirty and would be cancelled the following year. Only One Day at a Time (in its second season) made a showing at #8, While One Day at a Time and The Jeffersons would both enjoy a healthy network run into the mid-eighties, it was evident that viewer tastes were changing.

Like season five, this season starts out with three multi-part storylines which allows these stories a little more room to breathe and not feel rushed. The Bunkers were no strangers to temptation as evidenced in episodes like **The Threat** from season three and the season five story **Edith's Friend** however Archie and Edith's relationship is shaken to its core in the season premiere **Archie's Brief Encounter**. At a neighborhood diner, Archie flirts with a waitress Denise (played by Janis Paige). He takes a lot of ribbing from his buddies that since she is reciprocating, there is no reason for him to have a little something on the side. He succumbs to his insecurities, caves in to their pressure, and takes Denise's number. When Archie returns home, he wants a quiet romantic night at home with Edith and winds up feeling lonely and left out as she runs off to take care of something at the Sunshine Home. Out of loneliness, he gives Denise a call and asks to stop by. Archie Bunker must be the worst philanderer in history as he stumbles his way to get into her apartment while maintaining a childlike innocence about his situation. It is evident he is having a crisis of conscience yet he pushes ahead, going so far as to claim a chair of hers for his own when he visits. Denise says all the right things to soothe Archie that he feels his relationship with Edith is currently lacking and within time, the two of them are dancing as Archie serenades her with a song he learned in France during World War Two. They embrace and kiss. Just about that time Carlos, a Puerto Rican delivery boy from Kelcy's, arrives with some beer. He finds Archie hiding behind the door and Archie clumsily tries to explain why he is there. Carlos tells Archie "Listen. Big deal, who cares? I don't care. Nobody cares no more. Why should you?" and leaves. While Archie has always felt superior, it is Carlos who perhaps teaches Archie the greatest lesson in this moment and saves him from making an even bigger mistake. Archie hastily leaves the apartment telling Denise it isn't a good idea they see each other again. Back home Edith knows something is wrong after she finds Denise's number that Archie has left by the phone. Archie tries unsuccessfully to lie his way through it eventually admitting to what he has done. A broken Edith leaves the house, telling Archie "The one thing I could always count on was you, now I can't count on you no more." Edith takes refuge at the Sunshine Home and Mike and Gloria arrange to have Archie and Edith over to the house to see if the damage can be repaired. Edith eventually returns home and they reconcile but not before she admits that the situation has made her stronger saying to Archie "I used to think that you was the only thing I could count on but that ain't true. There's something else that I can count on. Me!" They renew their vows to one another and embrace. Perhaps Edith took a page from her own book and followed the advice she gave Gloria in the season four-episode **Gloria Sings the Blues** and waited to recognize Archie again. The acting by Carroll O'Connor and Jean Stapleton is solid and honest as these two characters struggle to find one another again and we as the viewer are invested in the story and rooting for them. While the affair is handled in a comedic fashion, you are mad at Archie yet you feel sympathy for him. It breaks your heart to see Edith cry as she leaves the house but, in the end, you applaud her for finding herself and that inner strength to forgive. Archie may feel in the moment that he has lost something but he has gained so much more and it has made them stronger. The difference is felt how their relationship will be presented for the remainder of the series.

Archie has lost his job after working for 30 years in **The Unemployment Story**. Meanwhile, Mike has his first article published, which will give him more recognition within the teaching community. Wanting to celebrate his accomplishment, Gloria writes a new song to the tune of "Happy Days Are Here Again" and wants Archie to participate but he refuses. Gloria judges him before finding out what is going on and begins to chew him out saying that he is jealous of Mike's success. When Edith angrily cuts Gloria off and explains that Archie has lost his job, the family rallies around him. The anxiety from the situation leads to stress related 'impudence' for Archie. In one of the most memorable scenes between Archie and Edith, she tries to comfort him in bed but he explains that he's not himself and doesn't want Edith to start something he can't finish. She turns over and Archie puts his hand on her hand as the camera closes in on his face. Down at the unemployment office, an employee explains to Archie there is nothing he really can do for him and much like in the season two episode **The Insurance Is Cancelled**, he is only following "the system". Archie eventually interviews for a janitor position and is competing with a gentleman who has more qualifications than Archie. When Archie gets the job, the man climbs out on the ledge of the building and threatens suicide. Archie talks him off the ledge and that night as he is going to bed has a gallstone attack. This segues into the next two-part story **Archie's Operation** where he is admitted into the hospital to have his gall bladder removed. While the tone of the series has changed considerably since season six, this episode has the feel of an episode from earlier in the series. Archie has a rare blood type, AB negative and some blood is needed for during the surgery. The only one who has a match is a black doctor. We are reminded of the discussion Archie had with Lionel back in the season one episode **Archie Gives Blood** however five years later, while Archie still shows some concern, he does not protest quite as loudly. This event will come in handy for Archie next season. When Archie arrives home, Hank Pivnik pays him a visit and lets Archie know that he will be rehired at work – as the new dispatcher!

With Mike and Gloria out of the house, the Jeffersons long gone, and Irene Lorenzo leaving the neighborhood the previous season, there was nobody on the home front for Archie to spar with. Liz Torres was added to the cast as the Puerto Rican nurse Teresa Betancourt whom the

Bunkers take in as a boarder. She was first seen as the admittance nurse in part one of **Archie's Operation** and in the episode **Teresa Moves In**, she is now living with the Bunkers. There is no tension to the relationship for the comedy to play off of, only the opportunity for Archie to take pot shots at her ethnicity so the relationship never really builds to anything interesting. This one episode would be the only time the character shined. After that, she was not given much to do and quietly departed the Bunker's house by the end of the season. Torres would reunite with Sally Struthers 20 years later in The Gilmore Girls and its Netflix reboot Gilmore Girls: A Year in the Life.

In **Mike and Gloria's Will**, after a brush with death on the subway, Mike decides that he and Gloria will not leave Joey in the care of Archie and Edith if something were to happen with them. Gloria argues that she did not grow up like Archie but Mike stands firm on his decision in the event that Edith is not around to act as a buffer to Archie's views. This episode is unknowingly prophetic as in two more seasons, the Bunkers will take in a little girl to live with them whom Archie will wind up raising himself after Edith passes away.

In **Archie's Secret Passion**, Edith has bumped into some old friends of theirs from high school; Bummie Fencel and his wife Dolores. She invites them over and when Dolores is mentioned, it triggers a memory for Archie of a time back in high school when he fooled around with her while Edith was away visiting family. He gets nervous fearing that Edith will find out, especially when her and Dolores spend time talking together in the kitchen. While Archie's memory of the event is romanticized and his bravado is a bit overinflated, Dolores finds it hard to remember the 30 seconds they spent together. Once Bummie and Dolores leave, Edith admits to Archie that she knows and he does not necessarily need to share everything with her from before they were married. A relieved Archie embraces his wife at the same time she says that she does not have to share everything that happened either. The look of surprise on Archie's face as the episode fades out is priceless.

Holidays have always seemed to be a challenge for the Bunkers and when a friend of Mike's shows up for Christmas Eve in **The Draft Dodger**, this Christmas is not any different. Mike's friend David Brewster has been living in Canada for several years while avoiding the draft during Vietnam. Meanwhile Archie has invited his friend Pinky Peterson over for Christmas Dinner. Pinky's son Steve served in Vietnam and was killed in action. During conversation, Archie finds out that David fled to Canada during the Vietnam War and tells him he will have to leave the house. Mike steps in arguing for Archie to finally admit that the war was wrong. Archie has yelled before but there is something so unsettling and chilling about his delivery in this scene. "I don't want to talk about that war, I don't want to talk about that (rotten) damn war anymore!" he shouts. Is as if Archie is hesitant to acknowledge that the country he so proudly believes in and served in World War Two might have been wrong for its involvement. It is yet another brilliant piece of acting from Carroll O'Connor. Figuring his friend Pinky will bond with him, Archie asks him to share his opinion. However, the senseless violence of war has cost Pinky his only son. When Pinky acknowledges that both his son and David did what they felt was best, he extends a handshake to make a gesture of humanity over politics and would rather sit and talk to David than dismiss him. Archie is very confused and perhaps disappointed at Pinky's reaction and stands alone. He approaches the front door where he hears carolers outside, telling them if they don't move on, he'll call the cops. He closes the door as the camera pulls in on the wreath hanging which says one word – peace – and the episode fades. The line Archie screams was originally "Goddamn war" and when viewed, you can clearly see that the line has been looped. All in the Family had used that expletive before in the season four opener **We're Having a Heat Wave**, however with this episode airing on Christmas Day 1976, CBS felt it a little inappropriate to take the Lord's name in vain and ordered the line to be looped. While understandable, it does take a slight punch out of Archie's monolog which beautifully builds from a slow burn to a full outburst. At the time this episode aired, deserters who fled to Canada were subject to prosecution if they were to return to the United States. There are several references to that policy during this episode. The war in Vietnam was always a hot topic for All in the Family which reflected the tone of the country as well. By 1976, that tone started to slowly shift and then President Ford had granted conditional amnesty to deserters. It was an election year however and Jimmy Carter defeated Ford to become the 39th President of the United States. Carter ran in part on a campaign which would grant an unconditional pardon to all who had evaded the draft during Vietnam. On January 21st 1977, approximately one month after this episode aired, Carter took office and fulfilled that campaign promise issuing Proclamation 4483 (Granting Pardon for Violations of the Selective Service Act) on his first day in office amid much criticism. This theme would be revisited, to lesser effect, in one of the final episodes of Maude in 1978.

Edith has wondered before if Archie still enjoys her company (**Archie and Edith Alone** from season two and more recently **Edith's Night Out** from season six) yet the effects of his encounter with the waitress are still felt in **The Joys of Sex**. Unbeknownst to Archie, Edith has gone down to the diner where Denise works and can understand what Archie saw in her. She starts to feel insecure and unattractive and purchases a book "How To Be Your Husband's Mistress" in hopes of spicing up their relationship. When Archie finds out, he reassures Edith that while he saw flaws and imperfections with Denise, the Edith that he sees is the same beautiful woman he's always seen; no wrinkles, no imperfections. Similar to his declaration to Amelia's husband Russ in **Amelia's Divorce**, Edith is perfect for him and his reassurance is all she needs to hear. For critics of the show who only acknowledge how mean Archie was towards Edith, all they need to do is view the final moments of this episode to see just how much he not only loved her but needed her as well.

While finally making several appearances in season five, we have not heard much about Stretch Cunningham since. Archie finds out he has died in **Stretch Cunningham, Goodbye** and is asked to deliver his eulogy. Known as a prankster on the loading dock, perhaps the biggest joke Stretch delivers is in the afterlife when Archie finds out he was Jewish. His eulogy takes up the majority of the second act in this episode and is as funny as it is sad when Archie second guesses some of the jokes he himself may have told Stretch not knowing at the time he was Jewish. Reportedly, Stretch Cunningham would have figured in as a love interest for Edith had Carroll O'Connor not come back to the show and this episode was a way to ensure Stretch would never come back.

There are some brighter story moments for Mike and Gloria this season. When Gloria thinks she may be pregnant again in **False Alarm**, Mike blames her as he did earlier in the season six premiere **The Very Moving Day.** Similar to that episode where he is called out by Irene Lorenzo for having a double standard and refusing to get a vasectomy, Gloria criticizes him for the same thing here. When Mike refuses to get the vasectomy, Gloria tells Mike that she realizes Archie was right about him and he is a "phony bleeding-heart liberal." The thought of Archie being right about anything where Mike is concerned causes him to have a change of heart and he has the procedure. In **Mike, the Pacifist**, when a man starts to choke his wife on the subway, Gloria intervenes. When the man shoves Gloria aside, Mike's instincts take over and he knocks the man out. Throughout the series, Mike has approached violence the same way he has approached the liberation of women; he is all for protest and championing the cause until said cause has a direct impact on his life. Recall the season three-episode **Archie is Branded** where an almost identical situation that Mike has now experienced on the subway is presented as a hypothetical. In that episode Mike agrees that if someone grabbed Gloria, he would want to react violently but that would only be a reflex reaction. Not only has Mike reacted instinctively with violence, he admits to feeling good when he hit the man. The subject matter is very interesting yet the execution of the episode is a bit clumsy as Archie is reduced to a commentator; punctuating the action occurring around him with unfunny one liners. The lesson Mike has learned is a bit of a bitter pill for him to swallow. Still conflicted, the episode fades. Mike knows non-violence is still the answer for him however there is a bit of satisfaction knowing he used violence to stop a situation before it harmed someone he loved. We return to the theme of Gloria feeling intellectually inadequate for Mike in **Mike and Gloria Split**. Mike is again belittling Gloria as he did in the season five-episode **Mike's Friend**. They fight and Mike goes to spend the night at the Bunker's house. The second act is dominated by Mike and Archie having to share the same bed together. The timing and execution of these scenes are perfect and the interplay between Mike and Archie is reminiscent of Laurel and Hardy. Mike breaks Archie's cot and Archie suffers more indignity when Mike spills water all over him in bed. After Mike corrects Archie's grammar, Archie yells at him for acting as if he is superior to everyone around him. It is one of the few moments in the series where Mike has learned something about himself directly from Archie and he is grateful, giving Archie a hug before he leaves the room to return to Gloria. When Mike arrives home, he apologizes to Gloria and again they discuss her going to school to further her education.

The executive producer for season seven was Mort Lachman who previously worked with Bob Hope. Lachman would share script supervision duties with Milt Josefsberg and would remain the executive producer through season ten. Mel Tolkin and Larry Rhine act as Executive Story Editor this season and will continue in this role through season ten.

Carroll O'Connor would win the Emmy Award for Outstanding Lead Actor in a Comedy Series for this season. The show again would be nominated for Outstanding Comedy Series and Jean Stapleton would be nominated for Outstanding Lead Actress in a Comedy Series. The episode **The Draft Dodger** was nominated for Outstanding Directing and **The Unemployment Story** was nominated for Outstanding Art Direction. Rob Reiner and Sally Struthers were both nominated for Golden Globes but neither won.

Things were beginning to wind down for All in the Family with its creator wanting to conclude production before the quality of the show began to suffer. While placing 12th in the ratings overall, America was still dedicated to these characters and would find it hard to let them go. While nobody knew at the time that the series would continue for another 6 years (including the transition to Archie Bunker's Place), preparations were being made for what was conceived as the final season of the show as season eight would be the last for two of its co-stars.

season seven episodes

Archie's Brief Encounter (part I-one hour) 9-22-76
Archie's Brief Encounter (part II) 9-29-76
With Edith paying more and more attention to her duties at the Sunshine Home, Archie steps out and pays visit to a waitress to whom he has been flirting with.

Episode notes
- Film and Broadway legend Janise Paige plays the part of the waitress Denise. She will return in the season nine-episode **Return of the Waitress.** One of the last survivors of classic Hollywood, Paige died on June 2, 2024.
- Scott Brady returns for the second and final time as Archie's work buddy Joe Foley.
- Archie's buddy Whitey Monroe is played by Teddy Wilson. Wilson was all over television in the 1970s through the 1990s, appearing in such shows as That's My Mama, M*A*S*H, Sanford and Son (as well as playing the lead in its spinoff Sanford Arms), The Golden Girls, and Wings.
- Jason Wingreen appears as the bartender Harry Snowden.
- This is the first of six appearances for Andre Pavon as Carlos.
- While part one originally aired in a one-hour timeslot, it is split into two episodes in syndication. Oddly, on

162

the DVD release there is a small scene at the top of the first episode which is inexplicably missing yet can be seen in syndication.
- Edith makes the same face at baby Joey that she said she made to Gloria as a baby in the season six episode **Alone at Last**.
- Sol Kleeger is played by Harry Davis. He will be replaced by Phil Leeds in the characters subsequent appearances.
- This is the first episode to mention that Jimmy Carter is in office.

The Unemployment Story (part I) 10-6-76
The Unemployment Story (part II) 10-13-76
Archie is fired from his job and must face a world of limited opportunities because of his age and lack of education.

Episode notes
- We learn that Mike's favorite food is kapusta and veprovina which his mother used to make all the time when he was a kid.
- When Archie is at the unemployment office, he tells the clerk that he's the first one to sing the Star-Spangled Banner when "old glory" is raised however in the season three-episode **Edith the Judge**, he has difficulty remembering the words to the song.
- The clerk at the unemployment office in part one is played by F. Murray Abraham. Abraham won an

Academy Award for his work in Amadeus (1984) and can also be seen in Mighty Aphrodite (1995). Most recently, he played Dar Adal in the Showtime series Homeland and appeared in the Max series' The White Lotus and White House Plumbers.

- Jeannie Linero makes her final appearance on All in the Family as the grocery clerk in part two of this story. Linero previously guested in the season-one episode **Archie Gives Blood** and the season two-episode **Edith's Problem**.

- The part of Frank Edwards in part two is played by Gerald Hiken. Partridge Family fans will recognize him as Dr. Bernie Applebaum. He also portrayed Katz the Butcher in the sitcom Car 54, Where Are You?

- Ellen Travolta has a bit part in part two of this story. She is the sister of John Travolta and has appeared on the short lived tv series' Makin' It (1979) and Joni Loves Chachi (1982)

- The layout of Archie and Edith's bedroom is sparser in these episodes, most notably missing the big dresser next to the bed.

Archie's Operation (part I) 10-20-76
Archie's Operation (part II) 10-27-76
Archie checks into the hospital to have his gallbladder removed.

Episode notes

- Liz Torres makes her first of seven appearances in this episode as Teresa Betancourt.
- Archie mentions that his friend Tiny has died. Tiny was part of the poker crowd in the season six episode **Archie the Babysitter**.
- This is the second appearance in the series of the character Dr. Shapiro. He was previously played by actor Gene Blakely in part two of the season six episode **Birth of the Baby**. Here he is played by Milton Selzer who appeared in such films as Alfred Hitchcock's Marnie (1964). Martin had over 200 other film and televisions appearances including lab man Parker in the hit series Get Smart (1965-1970).
- It cost Archie $3,200 to have his gallbladder removed in 1976. In protest, he tells the doctor it only cost him $131.50 to have Gloria and he and Edith were able to take her home!
- Mike offers Archie $1,500 to get through his unemployment crisis.
- This is the first appearance for Danny Dayton as Hank Pivnik. Dayton's career includes appearances on The Phil Silvers Show (You'll Never Get Rich), Get Smart, and Columbo. He also directed episodes for Here's Lucy and the short-lived series Good Morning, World. Additionally, he made feature film appearances including the Jerry Lewis comedy

Which Way to the Front? (1970) which makes sense as Archie refers to Hank as the Jerry Lewis of the loading dock. Dayton would continue the role of Hank Pivnik when the series transitioned to Archie Bunker's Place in 1979.

Beverly Rides Again 11-6-76
Tired of being the butt of Pinky Peterson's jokes, Archie encourages Beverly LaSalle to accompany Pinky on a double date with he and Edith.

Episode notes
- Eugene Roche appears as Pinky Peterson.
- Jason Wingreen makes an appearance as Harry Snowden.
- Danny Dayton returns as Hank Pivnik.
- Andre Previn makes another appearance as Carlos.
- The foursome dines at Hop Sings which appears to have undergone a remodel since Archie and Edith last visited in the season six-episode **Edith Breaks Out**.

Teresa Moves In 11-13-76
Wanting to bring some extra money into the house, the Bunker's take on a boarder who just happens to be the admittance nurse from the hospital where Archie had his gallbladder removed.

Episode notes
- Liz Torres returns as Teresa Betancourt.
- Rob Reiner does not appear in this episode.

Mike and Gloria's Will 11-20-76
After a brush with death, Mike decides that if something happens to him and Gloria, he does not want Archie raising baby Joey.

Episode notes
- Gloria mentions the book William's Doll which was featured in segment of the Marlo Thomas special "Free to Be You and Me" (as a duet with M*A*S*H star Alan Alda)

Mr. Edith Bunker 11-27-76
Edith saves the life of a man who is having a heart attack during a visit to the Sunshine Home.

Episode notes
- Veteran actor Phil Leeds makes the first of two appearances as Sol Kleeger (old man Kleeger). Leeds can be seen in The Monkees, Barney Miller, and Ally McBeal among over 100 other film and TV appearances over a six-decade career.
- Liz Torres returns as Teresa Betancourt.
- Jason Wingreen appears as Harry Snowden.
- Danny Dayton makes and appearance as Hank Pivnik.

- Rob Reiner does not appear in this episode.
- The part of Kate Korman is played by Priscilla Morrill who makes her final appearance in the series. She can also be seen the episodes **Archie in the Hospital**, **Class Reunion**, and part two of **Birth of the Baby**.

Archie's Secret Passion 12-4-76

Edith invites an old friend of Archie's to the house for dinner when Archie discovers that he had a fling with his wife back when they were in high school.

Episode notes
- Although Edith says in this episode she has not seen Bummie Fencel in over 30 years, in the season two-episode **Mike's Problem**, Archie tells Mike that he bumped into Bummie on the subway.
- Sally Struthers does not appear in this episode.
- The part of Dolores is played by Estelle Parsons who co-starred in such classic films as Bonnie and Clyde (1967). Parsons went on to a recurring role on the hit series Rosanne. More recently she appeared in The Good Wife and the Netflix series Grace and Frankie. Parsons will return in season nine (and on Archie Bunker's Place) as Barney Hefner's wife Blanche.
- While in the season two-episode **Cousin Maude's Visit**, Edith recounts a story of meeting Archie at the

Puritan Ice Cream Company, here it is suggested that Edith and Archie went to the same high school together. However, in the season four-episode **Class Reunion**, it is evident that Edith went to a different high school as Archie is not part of her reunion.

The Baby Contest 12-11-76

Archie and Barney enter both of their grandchildren in the Flushing Tribune beautiful baby contest.

Episode notes

- Jason Wingreen appears as Harry Snowden.
- Danny Dayton makes and appearance as Hank Pivnik.
- Allan Melvin appears as Barney Hefner.
- Mike and Archie refer to the current Presidential election where Jimmy Carter defeated Gerald Ford to become the 39th President of the United States. Archie somewhat prophetically tells Mike the country is getting Ronald Reagan for President in 1980.
- While Barney enters his Granddaughter in the beautiful baby contest, there is never a mention or suggestion that he has any children or Grandchildren in any other episode.

Gloria's False Alarm 12-18-76

Gloria believes she is pregnant again and Mike makes the decision to get a vasectomy.

Episode notes

- Dr. Dolby is played by Michael Mann. Mann previously guested in the season six-episode **New Year's Wedding** and will return later in season nine as Rabbi Jacobs in **Stephanie's Conversion**.

The Draft Dodger 12-25-76

Mike's friend who dodged the Vietnam draft pays Mike a visit on Christmas Eve and is invited to dinner.

Episode notes

- The part of David Brewster is played by actor / director Renny Temple. Temple starred in the short-lived series The Life and Times of Eddie Roberts and made appearances on such shows as Eight is Enough, Soap, and Gimme a Break!. He also directed episodes of Head of the Class, Growing Pains, and Empty Nest.
- Eugene Roche appears as Pinky Peterson.
- Liz Torres returns as Teresa Betancourt

The Boarder Patrol 1-8-77

With Archie and Edith away for the weekend for Aunt Iola's 90th birthday, Teresa decides to spend the night in the Bunker's home with her boyfriend Brian Schlemmer.

Episode notes

- Liz Torres makes another appearance as Teresa Betancourt
- The black man who mistakenly takes Edith's bag in the bus terminal is played by Juan DeCarlos. He previously played the furnace man in the season four classic **Archie in the Cellar**.
- Brian Schlemmer is played by Patrick Cronin who can also be seen in Star Trek: The Next Generation and Seinfeld.
- The three doors on the Bunkers second floor seem to be interchangeable as needed for a particular episode. Here, Mike and Gloria's old bedroom, which is now Teresa's room, is on the left side of the screen and the bathroom is on the right. This would indicate that the door in the back of the hallway leads to Archie and Edith's room. Yet if you view the season three-episode **Battle of the Month**, Archie eavesdrops with a glass pressed up against the back wall of his room to hear the fight the kids are having in their room, indicated they share a wall. With the layout of the rooms as presented in *this* episode, he would have had the glass pressed up to an outside wall of the house.
- This is the first of several episodes where we Mike does not have a mustache.

Archie's Chair 1-15-77

Mike accidentally breaks Archie's chair and through a series of misunderstandings, it winds up in an art exhibit.

Episode notes

-   While Mike did not have a moustache in the previous episode (**The Boarder Patrol**), he makes a point in this episode that he has just shaved it off and Gloria reacts with laughter as if it is the first time she has seen him like that.
-   Actor Michael Pataki plays the artist Lichtenrauch. Pataki previously starred in the season four episode **The Taxi Caper** as Detective Sgt. Tony Roselli.

Mike Goes Skiing 1-22-77

Mike fakes being run down so he can sneak away with the guys on a skiing weekend.

Episode notes

-   Liz Torres appears as Teresa Betancourt.
-   Mark Lonow plays Mike's friend Peter Gavaris. He will return as Amy Bloom's father Barry in season twelve.

Stretch Cunningham, Goodbye 1-29-77

Stretch Cunningham dies and Archie is asked to deliver his "euro-ology."

Episode notes
- We find out in this episode that Stretch's real first name was Jerome.
- Mike writes the eulogy for Archie and it is one of the rare times where Archie acknowledges what Mike did for him.
- The part of Harry Moss is played by Jay Gerber who will return in the first episode of Archie Bunker's Place as Murry Klein's attorney Levy. He also appeared in several other TV shows including Barney Miller and Too Close for Comfort.
- The Rabbi is played by Charles Siebert making his second of three appearances on the show. He can also be seen in the season six-episode **Archie's Civil Rights** and the season nine-episode **Edith's Final Respects**.

The Joys of Sex 2-5-77
Fearing Archie has lost attraction for Edith, she reads a trashy self-help book to put some spice back into their marriage.

Episode notes
- Jason Wingreen appears as Harry Snowden.

Mike, the Pacifist 2-12-77
Mike is conflicted after he knocks a man out on the subway who shoved Gloria.

Episode notes

- Howard is played by Wynn Irwin who was featured on the short-lived Dom DeLuise series Lotsa Luck and guested on Hart to Hart and Barney Miller.
- Marcia is played by Nita Talbot who appeared in everything from The Monkees to The Partridge Family and had a recurring role on Hogan's Heroes for which she received an Emmy nomination as Russian Spy Marya Rarmanova.
- The part of the wino is played by William Pierson. He appeared in the World War II drama Stalag 17 and is perhaps best known as Dean Travers on the series Three's Company.

Fire 2-16-77

When a fire breaks out in the Bunker's bathroom, Archie tries to defraud the insurance company by making it look like there was more damage to the house.

Episode notes

- Liz Torres makes her final appearance as Teresa Betancourt.
- Allan Melvin appears as Barney Hefner.
- When you hear Barney's dog barking outside, you can hear Barney call him Sam, perhaps a nod to Melvin's character Sam Franklin on The Brady Bunch. In a few episodes his dog's name will be changed to Rusty.

- The part of the insurance adjuster Mr. Ligway is played by Roger C. Carmel. Probably best known to Star Trek fans as Harry Mudd, Carmel also appeared on Batman, and co-starred on The Mothers-In-Law among many other credits.
- In another continuity error with the Bunker's upstairs, the bathroom in this episode is on the left side with Archie and Edith's room on the right.

Mike and Gloria Split 2-26-77

Mike stays with Archie and Edith after he and Gloria have a fight.

Episode notes

- Although in the episode **Archie and the Kiss**, Archie gives the sculpture of The Kiss back to Frank Lorenzo, if you look closely, you can see it on the floor in the corner of the Stivic's bedroom.
- When Mike takes the cot to sleep on, Archie reminds him that his cousin Oscar died on that cot when he was staying there in season two.
- The layout of the Bunker's second floor has changed again in this episode. It appears that the second bedroom Archie and Mike are sleeping in shares a wall (again) with Archie and Edith's room.

Archie the Liberal 3-5-77

Feeling pressure from the local media, Archie's lodge – The Kings of Queens decide to take in a black member... who is also Jewish!

Episode notes

- Jason Wingreen appears as Harry Snowden.
- Danny Dayton makes and appearance as Hank Pivnik.
- Allan Melvin appears as Barney Hefner.
- Sally Struthers does not appear in this episode.
- The part of Solomon Jackson is played by James McEachin who can also be seen in the season three-episode **Archie's Fraud**. McEachon portrayed the title character Tenafly which was part of the NBC Mystery Movie anthology series. He also guest starred on many of the series' installments including Columbo, McCloud, and McMillan and Wife. He can also be seen in the 1971 Clint Eastwood classic Play Misty for Me.

Archie's Dog Day Afternoon 3-12-77

Archie accidentally hits Barney's dog with his cab.

Episode notes

- Allan Melvin appears as Barney Hefner.
- Tracy Bogart appears as the receptionist in this episode. She is the daughter of series director Paul Bogart and previously appeared in the season

six-episode **Grandpa Blues**. She will make another appearance in season nine.

- The name of Barney's dog is Rusty yet a few episodes earlier Barney calls him Sam.
- Archie wishes he had a cat to 'ball and throw it nails first' at Rusty yet doesn't reference the Bunker's beloved cat who hated Archie's guts. While never seen on screen, Arthur is mentioned in several episodes including **Flashback: Mike and Gloria's Wedding**.

SEASON EIGHT

Touted as the final season of the series at the time of its airing, the cast puts in some of its finest work highlighted by several dramatic story lines which showcase elements that many remember best about the series. Carroll O'Connor would stretch his dramatic wings further when he portrayed Frank Skeffington – along with acting mentor Burgess Meredith - in a Hallmark Hall of Fame production of The Last Hurrah which aired on NBC in November of 1977. With very few weak spots, this is a solid season and the show was moved again, this time to Sunday's at 9pm Eastern. Most of the episodes are again played as an ensemble which was the strength of the series. Rob Reiner and Sally Struthers are given some of their best material to work with and rise to the occasion. This all culminates in the emotional season finale when Mike and Gloria move to California. The audience responded and put the show back in the top ten; finishing the year at number four (tied with 60 Minutes and Charlie's Angels) and behind Three's Company, Happy Days, and top-rated Laverne & Shirley.

The season would not begin without another hint of drama from its star as Carroll O'Connor once again considered walking away from the show "I do not make nearly as much as stars of some other, less highly rated shows"[45] but after further soul searching decided to come back. "I didn't want to be the one to kill the show"[46] O'Connor told People magazine.

Bob Weiskopf and Bob Schiller come on board this season as script consultants. Weiskopf wrote for Eddie Cantor and Fred Allen before teaming with Schiller where together they penned over 50 episodes of the classic sitcoms I Love Lucy and the Lucy-Desi Comedy Hour as well as episodes of Maude and the Flip Wilson variety show Flip. In addition, they would contribute to over a dozen scripts for All in the Family in its final two seasons as well as eight episodes in the first season of Archie Bunker's Place. As a result, while dealing with intense subject matter in several episodes (**Edith's Fiftieth Birthday, Archie's Bitter Pill, Edith's Crisis of Faith**), the show has more of an old time feel to it like many of the scripts Weiskopf and Schiller were involved with in the 1950s.

When Kelcy has a heart attack, he decides to retire in the one-hour season premiere **Archie Gets the Business**. While paying Kelcy a visit Archie overhears that Harry is interested in buying the bar and decides he wants to do that as well. However, in trying to apply for the loan the only way Archie will be able to swing it is to put his house up for collateral (it was paid off in the season six finale **The Very Moving Day**) and must get Edith to co-sign for the loan. Edith says they are too old to start over. She tells Archie that with the house paid off, she finally feels secure since during the depression her father feared losing their home. Archie has tried to get ahead in many other episodes but this is his first legitimate shot at being a success. Archie recalls that when he was a child, he wanted a bike so badly that he would pick up an odd job here and there to raise the money. After two years of saving, his father came by and took all his money and said he was putting it in the bank. Archie never got the bike and it is suggested he never saw his money again. With Edith's lack of support for his dream, he again feels how he felt the day his father took his money from him. Archie winds up forging Edith's name on the loan application and he is now the owner of the bar. Of course, Archie will say he only traced her name when challenged. With Edith devastated that Archie would do something like that, support comes from none other than Mike. He recalls the conversation he and Edith had in the season four episode **The Games Bunkers Play** where she told him that Archie was jealous because Mike had all the opportunities Archie never had. Mike tells her that while forging her name was a terrible thing to do, Archie must have wanted the bar really bad to do something like that as it was his was his opportunity to better himself and be somebody. Telling Edith it's something she really cannot take away from Archie, Mike concludes that Archie will need her support and if he fails, he's going to need her support more than ever. It is another of many touching one on one scenes in the series where the usual chaos quiets down long enough for the characters to discuss or reflect on the events leading up to that moment. Rob Reiner and Jean Stapleton deliver strong earnest performances in this scene.

With nervous anticipation, Archie's Place opens in **Archie's Grand Opening**. Although we have not met Harry until the season six finale **Edith's Night Out**, he says he worked for Kelcy for ten years and resents the fact that Archie bought the bar behind his back. Tensions between the two come to a boiling point where Harry quits and goes to McFeeny's (soon to be) topless bar down the street, taking all of Archie's customers with him. The evening continues when Archie is visited by Mr. Sanders, the personnel manager from the plant Archie works with who threatens Archie that he needs to get back to work. With confidence that he is going to make it on his own, Archie tells Mr. Sanders he has quit.

With Harry and many of his customers now gone, Archie struggles in the two parter **Archie's Bitter Pill / Archie's Road Back**. His buddy Hank recommends a "pick me up" (speed) to Archie to get him through his tough time.

Soon enough, Archie is mixing alcohol and pills and is flying high. This does nothing to improve his situation. When the rest of the family visits him at the end of part one he tries to put on a brave face, rattling off all kinds of business ideas during a stoned monologue. His worst fears finally rise to the surface as he admits that he has no idea what he is doing. He resides to the fact that he is only a working man and should have listened to Edith. Edith embraces him and the family surrounds him as he finally breaks down in tears saying to everyone that he "didn't mean to do no harm." Edith needs to give Archie the support that Mike spoke to her about. Ashamed of his behavior, in part two he recovers at home as the family plans a reconciliation with Harry. Apprehensively, the two of them come to an agreement where they will be 60/40 partners and the business is saved as is the future of the series although it was not known at this time.

Hands down, the most unsettling episode of the season and the series is the one-hour **Edith's Fiftieth Birthday**. Norman Lear contacted Gail Abarbanel as a consultant for this episode. Abarbanel founded the Rape Treatment Center in 1974 after starting out as a social worked at the Santa Monica Hospital. After spending some time with a young woman in her 20s who was brought to the ER after a suicide attempt, it was discovered that the attempt was triggered by post-traumatic stress after the woman had been repeatedly raped one evening. As a result of this encounter, Abarbanel founded the Treatment Center since victims of sexual assault did not really have a resource to turn to in the 1970s. The script was originally conceived as a storyline for Ann Romano on One Day at a Time. All in the Family dealt with this topic in the season three finale **Gloria the Victim**, however Norman Lear felt that rape did not only occur to young women; any woman at any age is susceptible to this vile crime and it would have greater impact as a storyline for Edith Bunker.

In the episode, Edith is preparing for her surprise birthday party next door when a man posing as a detective asks to enter the house. Soon it is revealed that he is the serial rapist who has been targeting older women. Edith is assaulted and the scene is violent, realistic, and an uncomfortable watch for the viewer. The audience gasps as Edith is being attacked. When she is finally able to break free by smashing a burning cake in the attacker's face, kneeing him in the groin, and pushing him out the back door, the decibel level of the audience cheering and screaming as Edith runs out of the house is deafening. It is a powerful first act of television. Actor David Dukes, who gives a very chilling performance as the rapist, recalled "There's a moment where I did something – I tore her dress or something to where it was clear I'm not gonna be a funny rapist, I'm....a rapist and the audience (groaned)."[47] According to an interview published online by Emmytvlegends.org, director Paul Bogart took a different approach to filming the scene of the attack. Whereas scenes are normally shot in smaller takes then edited together for broadcast, Bogart chose to film the scene in one long sustained take. It pays off as the tension builds up until Edith finally escapes and the audience can release.

When Edith finally reaches next door and explains what has happened, Archie and Mike agree to go back to the house to make sure all is clear. The clumsy, slapstick like approach to them checking the house is in total juxtaposition to the tone that the first act has set. It can almost be forgiven though as it gives us, the viewer, a chance to breathe and recover. A police report is filed after the rapist was grabbed off the street but Edith refuses to go down and identify him. In the weeks that follow, Edith shuts down completely and refuses to leave the house. She feels she is somehow at fault and that Archie will not love her anymore. Meantime, the police have called the house as the same man has been arrested for a similar assault. Edith refuses to go down and identify him again as she is too scared. Drawing from her own experience in season three, Gloria tries to convince Edith that going down to the police station and identifying the man will help her to stop feeling victimized and take control back of her life so she will not feel scared anymore. Edith momentarily turns to leave then runs for the safety of her chair. Gloria berates her saying she is surprised that the woman she knows to be so loving, caring, and helpful to others would be so selfish. Edith covers her ears as Gloria yells that she is not her mother anymore. Edith defiantly stands up and gives Gloria a slap across the face. Breaking down, they hold each other and an apologetic Edith agrees to go down and identify this man. The episode was so effective, Rape Crisis Centers across the country showed it to convey what victims deal with because of this crime. Jean Stapleton turns in yet another incredible piece of acting in this episode.

Archie mistakenly gets involved with the KKK in the two-parter **Archie and the Ku Klux Klan**. When Archie complains loud enough in the bar about looting during a blackout, a customer overhears his ranting. Approaching Archie, he tells him he likes the way he thinks and asks him to join the Kweens Kouncil Of Krusaders. Meantime, at Archie's insistence, Mike has written a letter to the local paper to say the looting has roots in the socio-economic problems of the inner city. Mike receives an angry phone call saying they are going to burn a cross on his lawn. Archie unwittingly attends this first meeting and finds out that they are going to target Mike. When he tries to warn Mike and explain how he got mixed up in this, a horrified Mike and Gloria shut him out. As Lionel explained to Sammy Davis in the season two-episode **Sammy's Visit**, Archie isn't a bad guy nor would he burn a cross on anyone's lawn (yet Sammy retorts that Archie would probably roast a marshmallow if he passed one and saw it burning). Archie knows he needs to right this situation. When he returns for the second meeting, he says he pleads with them not to burn the cross because he does not want his Grandson Joey to get the wrong idea of what the cross represents. When that does not work, out of desperation he says he cannot join as he has black blood in him from the transfusion he received in the season seven-episode **Archie's Operation**. He warns everyone that he knows their faces and if they continue down this path, he and all his "black blood brothers are going to come back and bust (their) honkey heinie's." Archie comes full circle here. The Archie we first met would never dream of saying such a thing but after witnessing a birth of Puerto Rican child (**Archie in the Elevator**), the death of someone using violent means to combat prejudice (**Archie is Branded**), the birth of his own Grandson, and the kindness of a black woman to give him the blood needed during his operation (**Archie's Operation**), he is more enlightened. This moment is the summation of how words can manifest into violence. There are miracles and acts of kindness around him that have forced him, sometimes against his own will and sometimes unknowingly, to be a more active participant in the human race.

Edith, described by creator Norman Lear is "somebody who would react the way we would imagine Jesus would react...love for everything, love for anything...simple love."[48] Her faith in God is shaken up in **Edith's Crisis of Faith**, another classic Christmas episode. When Beverly LaSalle returns to invite the family for her big premiere at Carnage Hall, it looks like it will be a wonderful Christmas season for Edith who has become close with Beverly. On their way to the subway, Mike and Beverly are mugged. When Beverly steps in to help pull the muggers off Mike, they focus the beating on her when it is discovered she is a transvestite. Mike is saved yet Beverly dies of her injuries. When Edith hears that Beverly was murdered because he was different, she shuts down. She wonders how one of God's children could be killed only because of her gender identification. She refuses to go to church and is angry with God. Despite the struggles Edith has been through, her faith has never openly been challenged. She is the one character in the series who has been able to see people honestly and accept them without question. In this moment it is Mike who, despite his own beliefs, can bring comfort to Edith because he can reassure her without bias. He tells her maybe people are not supposed to understand such complex things all at once and if there is a God, "(Edith) is one of the most understanding people he ever made." It is such a warm scene between these two talented actors and another example of how the kids have grown during the series. From their experiences and the wisdom, they have absorbed through Archie and Edith, they can now return the favor and console them when needed.

Other episodes this season deal with more standard sitcom fare. **Archie and the Super Bowl**, which aired after Super Bowl XII (Dallas Cowboys vs. Denver Broncos), deals with Archie renting a big screen tv for the big game and the bar is held up. Edith is chosen to participate in a laundry detergent commercial but her honesty prevents her from keeping the job in **The Commercial**. We are treated to the last of the flashback episodes in **Mike and Gloria Meet**. In **Stale Mates**, the kids take a weekend vacation to try and rekindle their marriage. While things would be patched up at the end of this episode, there were dark clouds in store for the Stivics in season nine. In **Aunt Iola's Visit**, Edith's Aunt comes to stay with the Bunker's and it looks as if her stay will be extended much to Archie's chagrin. Iola is played by Nedra Volz, a go-to actor if you needed an elderly woman for your sitcom. However, like the other shows she appeared on (Diff'rent Strokes, Alice, One Day at a Time) she is given zippy double-entendre one liners that fall flat to a modern viewer. After a line is delivered, she sits there as if to wait for the audience to applaud and laugh which is more at home with the aforementioned shows than with All in the Family. Aunt Iola is a very active 90-year-old woman and Archie, as he has so many times before, fears her because it reminds him that he is getting old. His view of old age and hers are worlds apart however and the episode is saved by a charming scene at the end where he finally acknowledges her zest for life and admits he should probably make a few changes as he ages.

Edith befriends the neighborhood butcher in **Love Comes to the Butcher**. Not realizing he has feelings for her, Edith invites widower Mr. Klemmer over for an evening of singing whereas Archie would rather hide out at his bar. After some friendly joking from his friends, he becomes jealous and returns home, bringing Edith flowers. Edith sees such a kind and lonely man in Mr. Klemmer and the misunderstanding is resolved as he leaves. Archie takes a seat behind the piano and plays a little song while he sings to Edith.

Two episodes focus on Archie's past where we gain a clearer understanding of his upbringing. After 29 years, **Archie's Brother** Fred pays him a visit with some bad news – he will need bypass surgery in a few weeks. Entertainingly enough for Mike, Archie's brother Fred also leans a little too far to the left for Archie's liking as was hinted in the season three-episode **Lionel Steps Out**. These two men clearly have never communicated or shared their feelings about one another yet with a crisis on the horizon, it is a time to reflect. Fred brings their father's old pocket watch and gives it to Archie. Archie clearly cherishes this watch and we can see in his face that it brings back a rush of feelings and emotions. We learn that Archie's father was harder on him than he was on his brother. Fred got the house, the attention, and most of the love from their father. Archie many times not only defended his little brother but took a beating for him from their father. This type of hierarchy could be relatable to some viewers. Fred explains that their father never had to worry about Archie but thought Fred needed more guidance. Much like the living situation in his own home for the past eight seasons, Archie had to assume most of the responsibility to care for his family. When Fred leaves, the camera closes in on Archie who, with tears in his eyes, realizes how much time has been lost and how much more there is for the two of them to say to one another.

In **Two's a Crowd**, Mike and Archie get locked in the storeroom of Archie's Place. With a little help from a bottle of alcohol, they begin to discuss their fathers. We find that there really were not too many differences between them; both had bigoted and racist views. The juxtaposition between these two characters has never been more evident and shows that such language and attitudes are passed down. It makes a subtle statement that we are all responsible for either breaking or continuing the cycle of bigotry and racism. Mike knew those things were wrong and took his life in a different direction whereas Archie, perhaps to try and please his father because of the family dynamics, continued to support these views. Archie relays a story that when he was a kid one of his shoes became so worn out and since they could not afford to buy a new pair, his father made him wear a boot and a shoe. The kids would tease him and call him shoe-booty. As the conversation continues, we learn that even as a kid Archie would use racial slurs because that is what he heard at home. Mike tells Archie that his father was wrong for saying the horrible but Archie counters saying that a father cannot be wrong. Archie begins to describe a childhood with a father who brings you candy, throws you a baseball, and takes you for walks in the park while holding you by the hand. Choking back the tears, his tone changes when he continues saying that his father once broke his hand on Archie while hitting him and that his father would shove Archie in a closet for seven hours, all to teach him "to do good." As his monolog unfolds you realize that the earlier part of his memoires with the candy, the baseball, and the walks in the park, are just fantasy – the type of childhood he wished he had - and the horror of the physical and emotional abuse he describes was the reality of Archie's childhood. He believes or is possibly trying to convince himself that it was all done because his father loved him. He tells Mike that a son should love his father, because a father loves his son. Making his way to the floor, he falls asleep. The camera pans to Mike who has a drained look of shock on his face. It is perhaps the defining moment of their relationship as for the first time, he truly understands Archie. Taking a piece of cloth awning, Mike acts as the father taking care of Archie the son and covers him up. "Goodnight shoe-booty" he says as the episode fades. Apart from exchanging their goodbyes in the season finale, this is the last time these two characters will have quality time together to explore their relationship to any degree of depth and the episode does not disappoint; it is one of the highlights of the series.

The season wraps up as the series began, with the focus on the four principal characters with little involvement from the outside world. When Mike takes a job as an Associate Professor in California in **Mike's New Job**, he and Gloria make their preparations to move. While Archie has talked before about moving to the West Coast in the season two episode **The Blockbuster**, now with the thought of losing his daughter, son-in-law, and Grandson, he denounces the state. Unfortunately, they must vacate their house as George Jefferson has sold it to a family of midgets(!). Mike and Gloria move back in with the Bunker's for their final two weeks in **The Dinner Guest** however feelings are hurt and tempers flare when Mike and Gloria decide to have dinner with Mike's new boss on their last night in town instead of spending it with Archie and Edith – who has cooked a special farewell meal for them. Finally, **The Sticks Go West** and when the day to leave arrives Mike confesses to Archie that despite their differences, he always was like a father to him. Not wanting to show emotion and remain the strong patriarch of the family, Archie continues to change the subject whenever the emotion of the moment closes in on him; if he ignores it, it is not happening. Edith has no problems in expressing her emotions when saying goodbye to everyone and leaves Archie and Mike on the porch alone. Mike confesses to

Archie "I know you always thought I hated you but I love you" and gives Archie a hug. With a shocked look on his face, Archie continues to hold back his emotions with some small talk and gently puts his arms around Mike, who continues to weep on Archie's shoulder. Archie goes back in the house and pulls the curtain back as we hear the door of the cab close. We cut to Edith whose hands are clasped over her chest as the taxi drives away. She leaves the room to get Archie a beer and it is only in this moment that Archie, finally alone, breaks down and cries. She respects his moment, returns to her chair and the two say no words to each other. They just stare in the distance as the camera pulls away. The stage darkens and the scene fades.

Norman Lear told People magazine that he "found it difficult to exit the series with anything but an admitted "shameless tearjearker""[49] O'Connor observed, "The last week of shooting was hard on Norman and the kids. I had doubts that we could get through it. Jean and I were hurting, too, because the people we loved were leaving."[50]

Many aficionados of the series believe the show should have ended right here, and for many it did, including its creator Norman Lear who announced that season eight would be his last of any direct involvement with the series. Perhaps on the strength of it being the last season for Rob Reiner and Sally Struthers, All in the Family returned to the top ten and finished fourth in the ratings for the year. Still profitable for the network, CBS wanted the show to return for a ninth season. With Norman Lear's blessing and a lot of money thrown at the stars from the network, Carroll O'Connor and Jean Stapleton would return for a retooled version of the show as they take on the responsibility of taking care of Edith's niece Stephanie.

The show would receive nine Emmy nominations and would win for Outstanding Comedy Series. Carroll O'Connor, Jean Stapleton, and Rob Reiner all would win in their respective categories as well. Paul Bogart received an Emmy for Outstanding Directing for the episode **Edith's Fiftieth Birthday**, and the writers for the episode **Cousin Liz** would also take home an award. The Golden Globes would acknowledge All in the Family as the best television series of 1978 with Carroll O'Connor and Jean Stapleton each receiving nominations.

season eight episodes

Archie Gets the Business (one hour) 10-2-77
Archie buys Kelcy's bar.

Episode notes
- The role of Tommy Kelsey (spelled as such in the end credits) is played by Frank Maxwell. Maxwell

appeared in such TV series as The Munsters, The Love Boat, and the soap opera General Hospital.

- Jason Wingreen appears as Harry Snowden.
- Kelcy's is being sold for $40,000 with $20,000 down.
- Archie and Edith only have $1,972.43 in their savings account.
- Archie claims he was once offered $47,500 for his house yet in the season two episode **The Blockbuster**, he is only offered $35,000
- Archie says the house is made of stucco and wood however in the season five-episode **Archie's Contract**, Mike notes that the house is made of brick (even though all exteriors of the Bunker's house show that it is wood).
- Andre' Pavon returns as Carlos.
- The role of the loan officer Ms. Watson is played by Norma Donaldson. She will return in the series opener of Archie Bunker's Place in 1979.
- When Archie shares the story about raising money for the bike as a kid, he mentions that his father called him a meathead.

Cousin Liz 10-9-77
Edith and Archie attend her cousin's funeral and learn she was a lesbian.

Episode notes

- Archie still has the yamaka in his suit from the season seven episode **Stretch Cunningham, Goodbye**.
- Edith's tea set has been in the family for 100 years.
- Archie mentions selling the tea set and taking a trip to California. He has thought of this location as an ideal place to live in such episodes as **The Blockbuster** from season two yet will denounce the state later in the season when Mike and Gloria announce they are moving there.
- Rob Reiner and Sally Struthers do not appear in this episode.

Edith's Fiftieth Birthday (one hour) 10-16-77

On her fiftieth birthday, a serial rapist attacks Edith.

Episode notes

- We can see in the close-up of the phone that the Bunker's home phone number is 555-7382.
- Sybil Goolie is played by Jane Connell in this episode. While Edith suggests in the season five-episode **Archie Is Missing**, that Sybil has a crush on Archie, here she is clearly annoyed with him. Connell appeared on many TV programs including Green Acres, That Girl, and Bewitched.

- The part of the rapist Lambert is played by David Dukes. Dukes appeared in almost 100 different television roles including series' Ally McBeal, Dawson's Creek, Law & Order, and the mini-series War and Remembrance. Dukes passed away on October 9, 2000
- The name of Mike and Gloria's goldfish is Mr. Jaws.
- While originally aired in a one-hour timeslot, this episode is split into two parts in syndication and on the 2011 DVD release from Shout! Factory.

Unequal Partners 10-23-77

Edith commits to holding a wedding in the Bunker home on the same morning Archie wants to leave for a fishing trip.

Episode notes

- Allan Melvin appears as Barney Heffner.
- Jason Wingreen appears as Harry Snowden.
- We learn in this episode that Edith originally wanted to name Gloria Jeanette after her favorite actress Jeanette McDonald.
- In the season two-episode **Sammy's Visit**, Barney is apparently married to a woman named Mabel. At the beginning of **Unequal Partners**, Archie refers to Mabel but Barney says he is with Blanche now. While we have never seen either Mabel or Blanche, we will get to meet Blanche in season nine.

- Musical rooms! In this episode, Archie and Edith's room is right across the hall from Mike and Gloria's old room.

Archie's Grand Opening 10-30-77

Archie's Place has its grand opening however everyone bails on Archie when he gets a little too bossy.

Episode notes
- This episode features Jason Wingreen as Harry Snowden.
- Andre Pavon makes his final appearance as Carlos.
- Allan Melvin returns as Barney Heffner.
- Danny Dayton makes another appearance as Hank Pivnik.
- Sorrell Booke makes his final appearance as Mr. Sanders.

Archie's Bitter Pill (part I) 11-16-77
Archie's Road Back (part II) 11-23-77

After struggling with the launching of Archie's place, Archie gets addicted to speed.

Episode notes
- This story arc was co-written by William C. Rader MD. Rader was introduced to Sally Struthers by Carrol O'Connor and the two would wed in December if 1977. They would divorce in 1983.

- Versatile actor A Martinez makes his sole appearance in the series as Manuel in these episodes. Martinez can also be seen in such series as The Streets of San Francisco, Profiler, Longmire, and more recently the Netflix series Avatar: The Last Airbender.
- Allan Melvin appears as Barney Heffner.
- Danny Dayton makes an appearance as Hank Pivnik.
- Jason Wingreen returns as Harry Snowden.
- In the second part of this story, Archie tells Edith she should have married Alvin Henderson who turned out to be a successful plumber.

Archie and the Ku Klux Klan (part I) 11-27-77
Archie and the Ku Klux Klan (part II) 12-4-77
Archie inadvertently is recruited to join the KKK.

Episode notes
- Danny Dayton makes an appearance as Hank Pivnik.
- Jason Wingreen appears as Harry Snowden.
- The part of Gordie Lloyd is played by Dennis Patrick who guested on the season five-episode **Archie's Contract**.
- Mitch Turner is played by Roger Bowen. Bowen appeared in many television shows and movies

and is recognizable to M*A*S*H fans as the original Henry Blake in the 1970 feature film.
- When Gordie approaches Archie in the bar, he says they used to work together yet we have never heard Archie mention him before. Gordie tells Archie he saw his editorial rebuttal on gun control, referencing the season two-episode **Archie and the Editorial**.

Flashback: Mike and Gloria Meet 12-11-77

Mike and Gloria reminisce about the first time they met one another.

Episode notes
- In the flashback sequences, the living room is laid out a little differently and Archie's chair is made of different material.
- Mike mentions to his college roommate that he is supposed to go picket the Nixon inaugural at the Waldorf.
- Mike's college roommate is played by Christopher Guest. Guest would attain cult status when he co-starred in the Rob Reiner classic mock-umentary This Is Spinal Tap (1984). More recently he is known for his send-up's such as Best in Show (2000) and A Mighty Wind (2003).

Edith's Crisis of Faith
(part I 12-18-77 / part II 12-25-77)
Beverly LaSalle is murdered which shakes up Edith's faith in God.

Episode notes
- Lori Shannon makes his final appearance as Beverly LaSalle.
- Allan Melvin appears as Barney Heffner.

The Commercial 1-8-78
Edith is hired to do a commercial for laundry detergent.

Episode notes
- The part of Mr. Prescott is played by Frank Aletter. He appeared on many other television shows including M*A*S*H, Police Woman, and Kojak.
- Darryl Hickman appears as flamboyant director Peter Grey. Hickman is the brother of Dwayne Hickman and has a career dating back to the late 1930s where he was featured in such MGM productions as Men of Boys Town (1941) and The Human Comedy (1943). His most recent acting credit is the final episode of The Nanny from 1999.

Archie and the Super Bowl 1-15-78
Archie's Place is robbed during a Super Bowl party.

Episode notes

- Allan Melvin appears as Barney Heffner.
- Danny Dayton makes an appearance as Hank Pivnik.
- Jason Wingreen returns as Harry Snowden.
- Gloria LeRoy returns as Mildred "Boom Boom" Turner whom we first met in the season five-episode **Archie is Missing**. She also starred as Bobbi Jo Loomis in the season three-episode **The Threat**.
- Louis Gus plays Sam. He can also be seen as one of the delivery men in the season three episode **The Locket**.
- Art Metrano portrays the other robber Jack in this episode. Metrano has enjoyed a long career in television in everything from Kojak to the Chicago Teddy Bears and co-starring in Joni Loves Chachi. He may be best known for his appearances in the Police Academy film series and its television spin-off.

Aunt Iola's Visit 1-22-78

Edith's Aunt spends some time with the Bunker's.

Episode notes

- Aunt Iola is played by Nedra Volz who also appeared on Diff'rent Strokes, The Commish, and Gimme a Break in addition to over 60 other film and television shows.

Love Comes to the Butcher 2-5-78

Edith innocently attracts the affections of a lonely widowed butcher.

Episode notes

- Jason Wingreen appears as Harry Snowden.
- Allan Melvin returns as Barney Hefner.
- The part of the butcher (Mr. Klemmer) is played by celebrated actor Theodore Bikel. He created the role of Captain Von Trapp on Broadway as part of the original cast of The Sound of Music and was also featured in the 1951 Humphrey Bogart, Katherine Hepburn film The African Queen.

Two's a Crowd 2-12-78

Locked in the storeroom at Archie's Place, Mike and Archie share a bottle and exchange stories of their fathers.

Episode notes

- Jean Stapleton and Sally Struthers do not appear in this episode.
- While Mike recollects that he knew his own father's racism was wrong, we learn in the season three-episode arc **Flashback: Mike and Gloria's Wedding** that his father died when Mike was very young. Raised by his Uncle Casimer who is portrayed as a guy who was pretty in touch with the world around him, would Mike really have such strong recollections of his own father?

Stalemates 2-19-78

After seeing how much their two friends Bob and Lorraine are still in love, Mike and Gloria take a getaway weekend to the Poconos to rekindle their marriage.

Episode notes

- The part of Mike and Gloria's friend Bob is played by Terry Kiser. With almost 150 film and television credits, he may be best known as the title character in the 1989 cult classic Weekend at Bernie's.

Archie's Brother 2-26-78

Archie's brother pays him a visit after a 29-year silence and has some bad news to share.

Episode notes

- Danny Dayton makes an appearance as Hank Pivnik.
- Jason Wingreen returns as Harry Snowden.
- This is the first appearance of Richard McKenzie as Archie's brother Fred. He will return in season nine and in the final season of Archie Bunker's Place. McKenzie appeared in many television shows including Soap, The Golden Girls, and reunited with Carroll O'Connor in his series In the Heat of the Night.
- We learn that Archie's father was a brakeman on the Long Island Railroad.

- While Archie has made mention of having a brother Phil and sister Alma in the season two premiere **The Saga of Cousin Oscar**, his brother's name changed to Fred in season three's **Lionel Steps Out** and we never hear mention of his sister again. By the season six-episode **Archie Finds a Friend**, he says he is an only child.
- When Archie and his brother discuss their father's death it is suggested it happened some time ago especially since he and his brother have been estranged for 29 years. However, in the very first episode of the series **Meet the Bunkers**, Archie mentions that both of his parents visited the year before.

Mike's New Job 3-5-78
Mike accepts a job as associate professor in California.

Episode notes
- Mike will be paid $21,800 at his new job.
- Archie makes the same declaration about having a goldfish in this episode as he did in **Edith's Fiftieth Birthday**.
- Sherman Hemsley makes an appearance as George Jefferson.

The Dinner Guest 3-12-78

Mike and Gloria move back in with Archie and Edith only to slight them on their last evening home by accepting a dinner invitation with Mike's new boss.

Episode notes

- The shaving scene at the beginning of the episode in the Bunker's cramped bathroom is reminiscent of the scene in the 1934 W.C. Fields comedy classic It's a Gift.

The Stivics Go West 3-19-78

Mike and Gloria leave for California.

Episode notes

- Clyde Kusatsu makes his second appearance as Reverend Chong. Kusatsu has close to 300 appearances to his credit including guest spots on M*A*S*H, Kung Fu, and most recently the Showtime series Dice and the Netflix series Avatar: The Last Airbender.
- Musical Rooms! Again, in this episode Archie and Edith's room is right across the hallway from Mike and Gloria's.
- Archie and Edith mention going to California in a year to visit the kids which is exactly what they will do when the Christmas episode of season nine rolls around.

SEASON NINE

With the departure of Rob Reiner and Sally Struthers, Carroll O'Connor and Jean Stapleton bravely marched into the final season of All in the Family. The episodes overall have more of a sentimental than dramatic tone to them, foreshadowing sitcoms of the 1980s in the way subject matter is dealt with. Season nine looks like a series that was influenced by All in the Family. The stories lack the edge which made the show a success yet on their own they still hit the mark on several occasions. Whereas close-ups would be used in past seasons sparingly to punctuate a scene, there is an overabundance of them in this season as a means of delivering the stories and they become more cloy and less effective. With the absence of Mike and Gloria, much of the action shifts over to the bar with supporting characters such as Harry, Barney, and Hank filling the void to provide comedy. This combination gives the show more of an old-time sitcom feel to it than ever before. Archie now sports a windbreaker most of the time instead of his beloved lumberjack coat and his main source of news is from the National Enquirer. The Archie we met in 1971 has all but disappeared and season nine of All in the Family acts as one long pilot for Archie Bunker's Place.

The biggest change of the series this season is the addition of nine-year-old Danielle Brisebois to the cast as Edith's niece Stephanie Mills who has come to live with the Bunkers. Brisebois had appeared in a 1976 feature film (The Premonition), Kojak, and was a smash as Molly in the Broadway production of Annie when the producers hired her for the series. When a show adds a cute kid to the cast, it is usually a sign of trouble. Adding cousin Oliver to The Brady Bunch in its final season is probably the most cited example of this practice. However, All in the Family was not suffering enough in the ratings to have to win viewership. The addition of the character provides the duo of Archie and Edith with someone new to interact with who is related to the family. Brisebois is understated in her performances which is why her addition to the cast succeeds. She is not given any cute one liners or catch phrases nor is she camera conscious. There is an innocence and honesty about her scenes with Carroll O'Connor and Jean Stapleton and unlike many other child stars who have come and gone, she has genuine talent to back it up.

Up until now, All in the Family was always taped before a live audience however in season nine, things changed. The show would now be taped and edited first, then shown to an audience where their laugh track would be recorded for the episode. It allowed the actors and crew to work in more of a relaxed atmosphere than the grueling schedule of taping in front of an audience.

If there is any success to be found in season nine, it is on the strength of the characters. Archie and Edith have developed into a fine comedy team and it is their interaction that provides the only genuine laughs during the season. To watch them is to watch the timing of two well-seasoned pros who are so comfortable in their roles that the performances are effortless. Mary Tyler Moore, still a commodity from her self-titled show which wrapped in March 1977, premiered her new variety show Mary. Perhaps trying to recapture some past glory from the 1973 line-up, CBS scheduled it as the lead-in to All in the Family and both shows premiered on the same night. However, with the variety show format dying out, Mary failed to find an audience and was removed from the schedule after three weeks. It would be revamped and returned to the network in March of 1979 but would be axed for good eleven weeks later. With the lead-in timeslot now vacant and the family viewing hour rules somewhat relaxed, All in the Family moved once again to the top spot of the schedule. Except for Good Times which was now in its final season, CBS gathered the remaining successful Norman Lear programs (One Day at a Time and The Jeffersons) and along with the non-Lear sitcom

Alice, built a new Sunday evening lineup. The audience was still responding to these characters and the show finished the season at number nine (tied with Taxi) and was the strongest showing of any extant Norman Lear sitcom by far. Meanwhile, shows like Happy Days, Mork and Mindy, Three's Company, and Laverne and Shirley (all ABC series) continued to dominate the ratings. Aside from network stalwart 60 Minutes, the only other CBS series to make a showing in the top ten was M*A*S*H.

The season kicks off with **Little Miss Bunker**. When Edith's distant cousin Floyd comes for dinner, he has an underlying motive – he wants to drop his daughter Stephanie off to stay with the Bunkers for a few weeks while he gets settled in Florida. When Archie refuses and throws them out, Floyd simply leaves Stephanie on their doorstep. As Archie and Edith unpack the situation further, they find that Floyd's motives are not as altruistic as they are presented. He has a drinking problem and has tried to leave Stephanie with other relatives yet nobody wants her. Stephanie tells Edith that her mom ran away with another man who did not want her. With Archie and Edith now empty nesters, they disagree on how to handle the situation. Archie loves the freedom they now have but Edith, perhaps now feeling lonely, loves the idea of having a little girl in the house again as it will keep them young and give her someone to dote over. Stephanie overhears this and leaves the house. A worried Edith calls Archie at the bar and asks that he tries to find Stephanie. He finds her in a bus station hiding behind a comic book and has a heart to heart with her about her situation. Archie finds out that her mom was killed in a car accident and the routine of abandoning Stephanie so she is put into a shelter is an all too familiar pattern for Floyd. Archie agrees to taking care of her for a few weeks. Their interaction is genuine without being saccharine and it is a beautifully executed scene between the two. Several episodes later in **What'll We Do With Stephanie?**, Floyd sends a letter to Stephanie which Archie steams open to read and learns that Floyd will not be picking Stephanie up. Similar to the way Archie fantasized about his childhood in season eight's **Two's a Crowd**, Stephanie embellishes the contents of the letter to Archie and Edith quite a bit so as not to make her father sound like such a heel. Archie places a call to the FBI to find her father and they send it to social services. A social worker visits the home where she deems the child will be well taken care of and have her needs met. Happy to know she will now be part of the Bunker's home; she joyously imitates Edith as she follows her into the kitchen to get Archie a beer.

Jean Stapleton receives a nice showcase in the episode **Edith's Final Respects**. When her Aunt Rose passes away, she wants to go to the wake. However, Archie refuses to go since Aunt Rose did not like him. When Edith arrives, she finds she is the only one who has come to say goodbye. In a monolog to her deceased Aunt, she tells her how wrong she was about Archie and what a wonderful husband and father he has been. She also laments how Aunt Rose never married even though she had opportunities yet chose to continue living life alone so she did not have to give up too much of her freedom. The life Aunt Rose lived left her with nothing except the final respects of one relative who has everything. The irony is not lost in the moment and Archie does wind up showing up at the funeral home to support his wife and escorts her home.

With increased screen time given to supporting players, we get several stories which focus on Barney Heffner. In **Reunion on Hauser Street**, his wife Blanche has run away with the exterminator again and by the time she sees the error of her ways, Archie has already fixed Barney up with Mildred "Boom Boom" Turner. She turns to Edith for support and with her guidance they reconcile. The reconciliation is short lived however in **Weekend in the Country**. When the Bunkers and Blanche escape to Barney's cabin for a relaxing weekend of fishing, Barney finds it hard to forgive Blanche for her affair. Again, Blanche turns to Edith for advice and the conversation recalls the discussion between Russ and Archie in the season five-episode **Amelia's Divorce**. Blanche suggests that she has quite the roaming eye when it comes to her marriage which has obviously caused problems.

She cannot understand what Edith sees in Archie and wants her to rate him as a lover. Edith innocently avoids all questions reassuring Blanche that Archie is all she needs in her life and after their discussion Barney and Blanche make up. Edith plays the role of the peacemaker in both episodes much the same as she did so many times in her discussions with Gloria. Finally in **Barney, the Gold Digger**, Blanche has left Barney once again. This time it is the furnace man. Archie and Edith decide to play matchmaker and sight unseen invite Edith's friend Martha Birkhorn. Martha is overweight and while Barney is initially turned off by her appearance, he eventually finds a connection and they date. Now the show could never be accused of being politically correct yet there are a lot of jokes that poke fun at Martha's weight and they come off more hurtful than humorous and pull down what is generally an amusing half-hour. It is not as if these episodes which focus on an ancillary character are void of entertainment, they are just not All in the Family.

Trouble walks back in on Archie in **The Return of the Waitress** when Denise, the waitress he had the date with in season seven's **Archie's Brief Encounter**, accepts a waitressing job at Archie's Place. There clearly is a chemistry still evident in their performances which adds a realism to the reunion. A short flashback of their night together is included and two agree to be mature about things and try to co-exist. When Edith shows up at the bar, Archie tries his best to have her avoid seeing Denise. Their paths do cross however (remember, Edith never confronted her but did tell Archie she went to check her out in the season seven-episode **The Joys of Sex**) and they sit and have a talk. They see what each other sees in Archie and Denise agrees to leave the job but not before Edith thanks her. Due to his encounter with Denise, his relationship with Edith changed and was stronger because of it. After Denise leaves, Archie approaches the table and to save face tells Edith he had to let her go. Edith does not let on that she knows he is making that up and whereas it is usually reserved as a dismissive insult to Edith, Archie tells her that she is a real pip for being so understanding.

The Holiday season begins with a very funny episode **Bogus Bills** where a sidewalk Santa Claus is passing around counterfeit $10 bills. It is nice to see a genuinely funny Christmas episode however, not to disappoint viewers, some sadness was just around the corner. In **The Bunkers Go West / California Here We Are** the Bunkers and Stephanie prepare to go visit Mike, Gloria, and Joey for the Holidays when the Stivics cannot come back to New York because Mike has thrown his back out. The injury is a ruse however when it is discovered that Mike and Gloria are separated. Gloria's fears in episodes such as season five's **Mike's Friend** and season seven's **Mike and Gloria Split** come to realization when the responsibilities of Mike's new job leave her feeling inadequate and underappreciated. For all their experience as a couple who was fully immersed in the counterculture movement of peace, love, fair-fighting, open mindedness, and understanding they learn they are not immune to the frailties of human fault and behavior. When it is learned that, because of her insecurity, she has stepped out on their marriage and begins seeing another man, Archie blows his top and the viewer is treated to a final act in this episode that reminds one the strength in these four actors playing off one another. When Archie hears the news about Gloria's new love interest, for the first and only time he sides with Mike against his daughter telling him "You're too good for her." Edith tells Archie that it is none of his business. Archie says that if it is not his then it must be God's business. Edith responds "Then you let God tend to it" much to the delight of the audience who applauds her reasoning. Edith again proves herself to be the emotional anchor of the family. Mike and Gloria admit to still loving each other enough to work on things. Edith and Mike leave the room and Archie finally admits that it is none of his business. He and his little girl embrace and tell each other "I love you."

Theodore Bikel returns as Mr. Klemmer in **A Girl Like Edith**. With the show now taped and edited before being presented to an audience to record the laugh track, this allowed the producers to indulge in a bit of camera trickery. Mr. Klemmer returns to visit the Bunkers with his fiancé Judith, also played by Jean Stapleton. Stapleton has an opportunity to stretch out and do something a little different and rises to the occasion. However, aside from the technical achievements of the episode the overall story feels more like filler and the results are flat.

The Bunkers find out Stephanie is Jewish in **Stephanie's Conversion**. The old Archie would have blown his top however here he is much more subdued and understanding telling Edith that they will just keep this to themselves. Edith goes upstairs to speak with Stephanie, who fears what Archie will think of her. In the season one episode **Gloria Discovers Women's Lib**, Edith has a conversation with Gloria in this very same room and explains her relationship with Archie saying "How do you know that what you see is all there is?" Now, in the last season of the show, Edith has similar advice for Stephanie telling her "Don't pay attention to what comes out of your Uncle Archie's mouth, it's what's going on in his heart that matters." Archie has always displayed a human trait which transcends his bigotry and prejudice; he judges harshly what he does not understand yet embraces one's differences when the situation is personalized (in many ways the opposite of Mike). Here he is no different as at the end of the episode, he presents Stephanie with a Star of David necklace explaining "You gotta love somebody to give 'em one of them. You gotta love everything about them."

Edith's job at the Sunshine Home comes to an end when she comforts a dying woman in **Edith Gets Fired**. The woman wishes to die and feels God is calling her but doctors keep bringing her back, her own daughter does not even come to see her. Wishing a peaceful death, she asks Edith to stay with her and hold her hand. It is a slight commentary on what happens when people age and decisions need to be made on their care. There is so much chaos on both sides that many times, the patient is lost in the shuffle. Edith is the only one there to understand what she wants and provides the comfort the woman needs as she passes away. Needing a scapegoat for the woman's very angry son-in-law who threatens to sue, Edith is discharged. Later, the woman's daughter pays a visit to Edith and now needs comforting from her. She wants to know what her mom talked about in her final minutes and Edith reassures the daughter that her mom loved her.

All in the Family celebrated its 200th episode on March 4, 1979 with a special 90-minute "best of" broadcast. What is unique about this is that hundreds of couples across 45 states were invited to the Dorothy Chandler Pavilion in Los Angles for the event which featured appearances by the four principal actors and Norman Lear.

In the final episode of the series, **Too Good Edith**, Archie prepares for a big St. Patrick's Day party at the bar. Edith has been diagnosed with phlebitis and is told to rest but does not tell Archie and proceeds to overwork herself to the point where she cannot walk. Dr. Shapiro is summoned and orders Edith to stay off her feet. Archie visits her up in their room and says he will take care of her. He lies next to Edith and holds her, telling her he is nothing without her. They embrace and Edith lovingly tells Archie that he is a pip, a real pip. They hold each other in silence as the scene iris's out, much like the end of a classic film.

Nominated for seven Emmy's (including Outstanding Comedy Series, Outstanding Directing and Writing for **California Here We Are**, editing for **The 200ᵗʰ Episode** and Outstanding Lead Actress for Jean Stapleton) only Carroll O'Connor and Sally Struthers would take home the Emmy this year. While nominated for Best Television Series and Best Actress for Jean Stapleton, the show did not receive any Golden Globes for its final season. With the odds against a nine-year-old series, viewers were not quite ready to let Archie Bunker out of their lives.

Audiences spent nine years with these characters and saw them and the real world they reflected change and evolve over 203 episodes. Sitting at number nine in the ratings and with a strong presence at the Emmys, CBS still saw the property as a moneymaker for the network and asked the stars to continue. With an OK from Norman Lear but no direct involvement, the show would indeed return for a tenth year however in a revamped version titled Archie Bunker's Place. More changes would be in store for Archie Bunker as the series and its main character devolved to the point where neither resembled itself.

season nine episodes

Little Miss Bunker 9-24-78
Edith's niece Stephanie comes to live with the Bunkers.

Episode notes
- There is a new opening credit sequence at the piano with Archie now sporting a sweater instead of his plain white shirt.
- The closing theme is slowed down a bit with Carroll O'Connor now announcing that "All in the Family was played to a studio audience for live responses."
- If you notice on the shelf next to the Bunkers phone, the photos of Mike and Gloria and Archie and Joey have been removed.
- Jason Wingreen returns as Harry Snowden.
- Although it is interrupted by audience laughter, in the scene where Edith gives Archie their home phone number, she says it is Ravenswood 86- -. When we see a close-up of the phone in the season eight-episode **Edith's Fiftieth Birthday**, it is listed as 555-7382. 555 is a standard prefix for television shows. "Ravenswood", at the time this episode

aired, would correspond to the main street that the Bunkers lived off, the first two letters corresponding to the first two digits of their phone number (in this case 72).

- Veteran television announcer Bern Bennet can be heard announcing the New York Islanders vs. Chicago Blackhawks game on the TV at Archie's Place.
- Chicago native Marty Brill plays Edith's cousin Floyd Mills. He will be replaced by Ben Slack when Floyd returns later in the season.

End in Sight 10-1-78

While getting an exam for partners insurance, Archie worries that a spot discovered on his liver might be cancer.

Episode notes

- The part of insurance agent Mr. Stanley is played by television legend Phil Leeds. Leeds previously portrayed Sol Kleeger in the season seven-episode **Mr. Edith Bunker**.
- When the Bunkers are going to bed, the song Edith sings to Archie is The Sun Will Come Out Tomorrow which was popularized in the Broadway play Annie – ironically, the play that brought co-star Danielle Brisebois to the attention of the producers.
- When Archie is talking to Mr. Stanley about various operations, he mentions changing a

man into a woman into a tennis player. This is in reference to Renee Richards who had male to female reassignment surgery and became the first transgender member allowed to play tennis competitively.

- Archie mentions that the Bunkers will take a trip to California in a few weeks.
- Archie affectionately calls Stephanie a little dingbat.
- Allan Melvin returns as Barney Hefner.
- Jason Wingreen appears as Harry Snowden.
- Danny Dayton makes an appearance as Hank Pivnik.

Reunion on Hauser Street 10-8-78

With Barney dejected after his wife Blanche runs off again with the exterminator, Archie fixes him up with Boom Boom while Edith tries to reunite the couple.

Episode notes

- Archie and Harry sing a line from the song New York, New York from the 1944 musical On the Town and it's 1949 film version which co-starred All in the Family alum Betty Garrett.
- Gloria LeRoy makes her final appearance on All in the Family as Mildred "Boom Boom" Turner.
- When "Boom Boom" originally visits the Bunker house in the season five episode **Where's Archie?** she clearly has disdain for him yet in her

subsequent appearances she has warmed up to him considerably.

- Estelle Parsons makes her first of two appearances as Blanche Heffner. Parsons previously guest starred in the season seven-episode **Archie's Secret Passion** as Dolores Fencel.
- Danielle Brisebois does not appear in this episode.
- Allan Melvin returns as Barney Heffner.
- Jason Wingreen appears as Harry Snowden.
- This is the first appearance of Bill Quinn as the blind philosophical patron of Archie's Place, Mr. Van Ranseleer although he does not have a speaking part and is not listed in the closing credits. Quinn had a lengthy career with over 200 credits dating back to 1923. Carving a niche for himself in episodic television, he can be seen on Perry Mason, The Munsters, I Spy, Mod Squad, The Streets of San Francisco, The Mary Tyler Moore Show, and The Golden Girls.
- When Edith asks Archie not to judge Blanche for her behavior, she reminds him of the waitress from **Archie's Brief Encounter**.
- We learn the waitress lives at 11364 67th St.

What'll We Do With Stephanie? 10-15-78

Stephanie receives a letter from her father telling her he will not be coming for her on the day he is supposed to pick her up.

Episode notes

- In the scene where Archie hands Stephanie the note from her father, notice how it is addressed to 74 Hauser Street, not 704.
- If you look closely to the front page of the Enquirer that Archie is reading you will see the cast of contemporary shows Alice and Three's Company.
- The Bunker's garbage can which is usually under the sink or next to the swinging kitchen door, is on the kitchen floor in this episode if only to be used to deliver the gag of Archie disposing the mail as Edith announces each letter one by one.
- If you look closely, in the scene where Edith tells Stephanie she can stay, the Bunkers couch is missing from the background (assumedly to allow for positioning of one of the cameras).
- The Bunkers finally catch up with technology in this episode and have a push button phone.

Edith's Final Respects 10-22-78

Edith turns out to be the only mourner at her Aunt Rose's wake.

Episode notes

- not only are these the final respects of Edith's dear Aunt, it is the last time we hear a reference to the Bunker's dearly departed cat Arthur (whom Archie hated).

- this is the last time we will hear in the series that Archie has borrowed Munson's cab.
- Charles Siebert makes his final appearance on All in the Family as the young man who mistakenly walks into the funeral chapel of Edith's Aunt. Siebert previously appeared as the Rabbi in the season seven-episode **Stretch Cunningham, Goodbye** and the season six-episode **Archie's Civil Rights**. He had a recurring role on One Day at a Time as Jerry Davenport and will go on the following season to portray Dr. Stanley Riverside II in the M*A*S*H spinoff Trapper John, M.D.
- Soft spoken character actor Howard Morton plays the funeral director. Morton would go on to such shows as One Day at a Time, Gimme a Break! and would portray Grandpa in the syndicated series The Munsters Today.

Weekend in the Country 10-29-78

Archie, Edith, Barney, and Blanche spend a weekend in Barney's cabin only to have old wounds reopened about Blanche's affair

Episode notes

- This is the last appearance of Estelle Parsons as Blanche Heffner.
- Allan Melvin appears as Barney Heffner.

- This is the first episode where it is mentioned that Stephanie is friends with Amy Bloom.
- Although we never see him wear it much during the season, if you look on the coat hook next to the Bunker's room in the cabin, you will see Archie's lumberjack jacket hanging there.

Archie's Other Wife 11-5-78

While on a wild weekend with Archie's army buddies, they pull a prank on him and make him think he has had an affair with a black woman.

Episode notes
- Allan Melvin appears as Barney Heffner.
- Danny Dayton appears in this episode as Hank Pivnik.
- This is the final appearance of Eugene Roche as Pinky Peterson. He previously appeared in **Beverly Rides Again** from season six and the season seven episode **The Draft Dodger**. Roche had many other television appearances including Quincy M.E., Murder, She Wrote, a recurring role on Soap, and as the dishwasher in commercials for Ajax Dishwashing Liquid. His final television role was in an episode of 7th Heaven in 2004. He passed away on July 28th of that year.
- Marabel is played by Jonelle Allen. Allen also made appearances on Trapper John M.D., Cagney and

Lacey, Dr. Quinn, Medicine Woman, and most recently in a 2017 episode of the Showtime series Shameless.

- Hank is played by veteran character actor Harvey Lembeck making his second (and final) appearance on the show. Lembeck previously guested in the season three-episode **Class Reunion**.

Edith Versus the Bank 11-19-78

Edith tries to get a loan from the bank to buy Archie a new TV for their anniversary.

Episode notes

- This is the third time the Bunker's need their TV replaced during the series. Either Archie is too rough on them or they were made more poorly in the 1970's.
- Edith mentions she has a total of $78 in her three accounts at the bank; her college fund for Joey, her Christmas Club account, and her potato cutter account.
- Edith says she makes $2.65 an hour at the Sunshine home. She must have received a raise as in the season six-episode **Edith Steps Out**, she is hired for $2 an hour.
- Edith originally goes to Kressler's to buy the TV but is refused credit because she is a woman. You would think that after the shoddy discrimination her

daughter experienced from being pregnant in the season six-episode **Mike Faces Life**, the family would be either be done with Kressler's or they would treat them a little better.
- John Harkin plays Mr. Faraday. Harkin also appeared on Alice, Taxi, and the Paul Newman feature Absence of Malice (1981) among over 70 other film and television credits.

The Return of the Waitress 11-26-78

Denise returns to Archie's life as the new waitress at Archie's Place.

Episode notes
- Janis Paige makes her final appearance as Denise.
- footage from **Archie's Brief Encounter** is incorporated into this episode in a flashback sequence.
- Danny Dayton appears as Hank Pivnik.
- Jason Wingreen makes another appearance as Harry Snowden.
- Bill Quinn makes an appearance as Mr. Van Ranseleer.

Bogus Bills 12-3-78

Santa Claus visits Archie's Place and gifts him counterfeit $10 bills.

Episode notes

- Danny Dayton appears as Hank Pivnik.
- Jason Wingreen makes another appearance as Harry Snowden.
- Bill Quinn makes an appearance as Mr. Van Ranseleer.
- Allan Melvin appears as Barney Heffner.
- Santa is played by John Finnegan who was also featured in episodes of McCloud and Columbo as well as the 1997 Chevy Chase comedy Vegas Vacation.
- Charles Hallahan plays the part of Officer Harrison. Hallahan can also be seen in the feature films The Fan (1996) and Dante's Peak (1997) among numerous other film and television credits.
- Sandy Kenyon makes his final appearance on All in the Family this time as Herb the police officer. He can also be seen in the season one episode **Archie is Worried About His Job**, and the season six-episode **Archie the Hero.**

The Bunkers Go West 12-10-78

The Bunkers prepare to visit Mike and Gloria when it is discovered the kids cannot visit due to Mike injuring his back.

Episode notes
- It is mentioned in the final episode of season eight that the Bunkers will make the trek to California yet in this episode, Mike and Gloria originally are going to come back East to visit the Bunkers.
- Allan Melvin makes an appearance as Barney Heffner in this episode.
- This is one of the few episodes of the season where Archie is wearing his beloved lumberjack coat.

California, Here We Are (one hour) 12-17-78
Archie and Edith arrive in California to visit the kids.

Episode notes
- Rob Reiner and Sally Struthers receive a special guest star billing in the opening credits.

A Night at the PTA 1-7-79
Edith accompanies Stephanie to talent night at her school.

Episode notes
- Jason Wingreen appears as Harry Snowden.
- Danny Dayton makes an appearance as Hank Pivnik.

A Girl Like Edith 1-14-79
After running into Mr. Klemmer at the laundromat, Edith invites he and his fiancé over for dinner. Only, his fiancé bears a striking resemblance to Edith.

Episode notes

- This is Theodore Bikel's second and final appearance as Mr. Klemmer.
- Jean Stapleton is billed as Giovanna Pucci in the part of Judith in the closing credits of this episode. The name is an inside joke; Jean roughly translates to Giovanna in Italian and Pucci is a riff on the last name of Stapleton's real life husband William Putch.

The Appendectomy 1-21-79

Stephanie requires surgery to remove her appendix.

Episode notes

- This is the first of two appearances for George Wyner as Dr. Sydney Shapiro. Wyner has appeared in almost 200 film and television roles including M*A*S*H, Matt Houston, Hill Street Blues, and a co-starring role on the short-lived series Kaz. He also played Colonel Sandurz in the Mel Brooks comedy Spaceballs (1987). More recently he has been seen on Shameless, The Big Bang Theory, and Grace and Frankie.
- The part of the nurse is played by Tracy Bogart, daughter of director Paul Bogart. This is her third and final appearance on the show previously seen as a nurse in the season six-episode **Grandpa Blues** and the season seven-episode **Archie's Dog Day Afternoon**.

Stephanie and the Crime Wave 1-28-79

Stephanie takes items from loved ones so she has things to remember them by after she leaves the Bunkers.

Episode notes
- Archie received his argyle socks from Gloria for Christmas.
- Mr. Ruskin is played by Davis Roberts. Roberts made several other television appearances including I Dream of Jeannie, What's Happening!!, and Quincy M.E.

Barney the Gold Digger 2-5-79

Archie and Edith try to play matchmaker after Blanche leaves Barney.

- Allan Melvin returns as Barney.
  The set of Mike and Gloria's house has been redesigned to serve as Barney's house.
- The part of Martha Birkhorn is played by Peggy Rea. Rea previously portrayed cousin Bertha in the season one-episode **The Saga of Cousin Oscar** and the season two-episode **The Blockbuster**. This is her last appearance on the series.

Stephanie's Conversion 2-18-79

Archie and Edith find out that Stephanie is Jewish.

Episode notes

- This is the first time Edith has mentioned Reverend Chong in relation to her going to church. Up to now it has been Reverend Felcher.
- This is Clyde Kusatsu's final appearance on the show as Reverend Chong. He previously appeared in the season six-episode **Joey's Baptism** and the season eight finale **The Stivics Go West**.
- The part of Rabbi Jacobs is played by Michael Mann. Mann previously appeared on the show in the season six-episode **New Year's Wedding** as well as the season seven-episode **Gloria's False Alarm**. He will reprise the role of Rabbi Jacobs in several episodes of Archie Bunker's Place.

Edith Gets Fired 2-25-79

Edith is discharged from the Sunshine Home after respecting the wishes of a dying woman.

Episode notes

- Danielle Brisebois does not appear in this episode.
- Barbara Cason makes her final appearance on the show as Miss Critchen. She previously appeared as Nurse Dorothy in the season six-episode **Birth of the Baby part II** as well as Clare Packer in the season two episode **The Election Story**.

- Mr. Johnson is played by legendary character actor Leonard Stone. Stone appeared as Doc Joslyn on the short-lived series Camp Runamuck and has also appeared on Perry Mason, I Spy, Mod Squad, The Partridge Family and nearly 140 other roles. Fans of Jerry Lewis will recognize him from The Big Mouth (1967) and Hardly Working (1980)
- Although she dies in this episode, Angela Clarke lived to be the ripe old age of 101 and appeared on St. Elsewhere, The Partridge Family, and Bonanza as well as the feature films The Great Caruso (1951), House of Wax, and Houdini (both 1953)
- Dolores Sutton plays Miss Critchen's daughter Norene and can also be seen in the 1987 Woody Allen film Crimes and Misdemeanors.
- Charlie Hammer is played by Michael McGuire. McGuire is known to Dark Shadows fans as Judah Zachary. He can also be seen in The Streets of San Francisco, Hawaii Five-O, Judging Amy, and JAG.
- Victor Killian had a rewarding career dating back to the late 1920s and can be seen in such films as My Favorite Wife (1940), Sergeant York (1941), The Ox-Bow Incident (1942), Meet Me in St. Louis (1943), and the 1946 Abbott and Costello film Little Giant. He was also featured in the Norman Lear series' Maude and Mary Hartman, Hartman. He will be

seen again in the penultimate episode of the series **The Return of Stephanie's Father**. Fans of The Brady Bunch will recognize him from the episode "The Treasure of Sierra Avenue".

The 200th Episode of All in the Family 3-4-79
A 90-minute retrospective hosted by Norman Lear which features clips from the series.

The Return of Archie's Brother 3-11-79
Archie's brother returns for a business opportunity for Archie to invest in Chinese food buffets but Archie's good mood turns sour when he finds out his brother's new bride Catherine is only 18 years old.

Episode notes
- At the beginning of the episode, Archie is in a much better mood hearing from his brother than in the previous season's episode **Archie's Brother**.
- Archie mentions that it would be so nice if he had a sister named Isabel forgetting that he apparently at one time did indeed have a sister Alma as mentioned in the season two - episode **The Saga of Cousin Oscar**.
- Fred mentions having only one daughter. We have already met Linda in the season five-episode **Lionel Steps Out** where she mentions Archie's brother has

raised five girls. We will meet the second of Fred's children – Billie - in the season three premiere of Archie Bunker's Place.

- This is the second of three appearances for Richard McKenzie as Archie's brother Fred Bunker.
- When they are in bed discussing the age difference between Archie's brother and his new wife, Edith points out that Charlie Chaplin married a much younger woman. Chaplin had returned to the US in 1972 after living in exile for twenty years to receive a special Oscar. He died Christmas Day in 1977, a little over a year before this episode aired.

The Family Next Door 3-18-79

The Jeffersons rent their house next door to the Bunkers to another black family…with Edith's help.

Episode notes

- Isabel Sanford makes an appearance as Louise Jefferson.
- Allan Melvin returns as Barney Heffner.
- Jason Wingreen appears as Harry Snowden.
- Janet MacLachlan makes her first appearance as Archie's new neighbor Polly Lewis. She will make a few appearances when the show transitions to Archie Bunker's Place. She can also be seen on Good Times, Cagney & Lacey, ER, NYPD Blue, and

will reunite with Carroll O'Connor in an episode of In the Heat of the Night.

- Character actor Richard Ward plays the part of Polly's husband Ed. This was one of Ward's final appearances in front of the camera. He is probably best known as Steve Martin's father in the 1979 comedy The Jerk and co-starred in the 1972 classic Across 110th Street. His final screen appearance was in the Robert Redford film Brubaker (1980).

The Return of Stephanie's Father 3-25-79

Stephanie's father returns to make a deal with the Bunkers in exchange for them to continue taking care of her.

Episode notes

- Victor Kilian returns to the series as the hotel clerk. He was previously seen earlier in the season as a resident of the Sunshine Home in the episode **Edith Gets Fired**. This was Kilian's final screen appearance. He died on March 11, 1979 before this episode aired.
- The part of Floyd Mills is played this time by Ben Slack. He will return to the role in an episode of Archie Bunker's Place. Slack guested on several soap operas in the 1970s and can also be seen in Happy Days, Remington Steele, Hill Street Blues, and the 1984 feature film Bachelor Party.

Too-Good Edith 4-8-79

While struggling with phlebitis, Edith pushes herself to cook for Archie's St. Patrick's Day party.

Episode notes

- This is the second and final appearance for George Wyner as Dr. Sydney Shapiro.
- Jason Wingreen appears as Harry Snowden.

"I regret nothing about my years on All in the Family except my own anger....I used to get angry about everything, even about ordering minor script changes....I refused to do situation comedy, the imposition of wacky plots upon the characters...I maintained that we were a satire. Satire is reality laced with ridicule. But the reality must never be eroded."[51]

Carroll O'Connor found himself optimistic and in a reflective mood in the Fall of 1979 when he penned those comments to TV Guide. Rebranded "Archie Bunker's Place", All in the Family returned to the air against seemingly overwhelming odds for a tenth year. It was moved up to the lead spot of the Sunday night lineup which also included the Norman Lear shows The Jeffersons and One Day at a Time and would remain in this slot for its final four seasons. It remained a top fifteen show until its final season where it – just barely – fell out of the top twenty all together, finishing at number 22. Norman Lear gave Carroll O'Connor the ok to continue yet was not involved in any of the creative decisions behind the show. The show would be produced through Lear's company Tandem along with the O'Connor – Becker Company, rechristened the Ugo Company in season eleven. Being one of the highest paid stars on television plus having more of a say in the creative development must have appealed to Carroll O'Connor yet without that strong creative voice in Norman Lear providing a counter argument, you really see how much that is missed in the creative process. While taping of the final seasons of All in the Family took place at Metromedia Square, production for Archie Bunker's Place moved back to Television City. Like season nine, it would be taped and edited yet the difference is, it was no longer played to a studio audience for reaction. Once completed, a laugh track would be added to each episode. This isolates the series and hurts its presentation a bit too as much of the energy always derived from an audience reaction and knowing the laughter we heard was real. In addition, the lighting of the Bunker's home is different. Many areas of the set are dark and give the house a flat, depressing, and claustrophobic look. The house loses dimension and it looks like Archie has not paid his electric bill. There would be no more Archie and Edith at the piano to open the show. The theme was given an instrumental reworking over shots of New York that eventually zeroed in on the storefront of Archie Bunker's Place.

From a storytelling standpoint, retitling the show made sense. Once the bar was purchased in season eight and with Mike and Gloria now gone, storylines started to gradually shift more over to the bar and its inhabitants. Season nine was somewhat of a test run for the format. Jean Stapleton was ready to move on and agreed to only appear four times. In the episodes in which she does appear, there is a certain something missing in her interaction with Carroll O'Connor as if she is there strictly as a favor to him and Norman Lear and goes through the obligatory paces. Apart from her final appearance (in **The Shabbat Dinner**) the spark is missing in her performances. Edith takes a full-time job in **Edith Gets Hired** which conveniently allows her character to be MIA from the majority of the tenth season episodes. With all of Archie's protagonists now gone, the shelves had to be restocked to give the character things to play off of and herein lies the problem with the final (roughly) third of the series.

Whereas in All in the Family, the world around Archie was more organic and grew out of the events the character experienced, in Archie Bunker's Place this world is more deliberate and shoved down his throat. At the end of the season ten episode **Hiring the Cook**, a defeated Archie sits with Mr. Van Ranseleer and rattles off all the changes in his life; a wife working full time, a new business partner who is Jewish, a new cook who is Irish-Catholic, and a waiter who is a homosexual. It is as if he is going down a checklist to make sure all vacancies are filled so that we the viewer are aware and the show can go on. Archie

Bunker is still the character we have followed for nine seasons but he is severely tamed, not changed and with few exceptions does not show the dramatic or comedic range he once displayed. All in the Family stood head and shoulders above the counterprogramming of its time. Conversely, Archie Bunker's Place rarely takes chances with its material and succeeds best when it calls back to the elements and themes which defined the original series. It is pretty bland stuff overall and the results stand in stark contrast to the observations made by its star.

O'Connor reflected in a story he wrote for TV Guide the week Archie Bunker's Place premiered "…it will be, as always, Archie Against the World, but the world will now be represented less by the family than by the characters in a New York bar and grill called Archie Bunker's Place. We think the battle will be nonetheless fierce and funny. We trust too that the world will still be strong enough to hold its own against Archie."[52]

Consistency is also a problem in the final four seasons of the show and hinders it from establishing an identity. All in the Family benefitted from a stable and tight behind the scenes crew during its nine-season run and in its final four seasons as Archie Bunker's Place, there are a lot of cooks in the kitchen. As talented as they all are, one would expect a more interesting output. Instead, the series seems at odds with itself. At season ten, Mort

Lachman and Milt Josefsberg who had guided the show since season six continue Production, Executive Script Supervision, and Script Consultant duties. Mel Tolkin and Larry Rhine return as Executive Story Editors however after season ten, these creative forces that guided All in the Family in its final seasons will leave.

Alan Horn served as Production Supervisor in season nine and continues those duties in season ten. He will assume Executive Producer responsibilities in season eleven and continue through season twelve. Horn continued work as production supervisor on other Tandem show such as Hello, Larry, The Jeffersons, Diff'rent Strokes, The Facts of Life, and One Day at a Time. Horn was Executive Producer for The Hobbit: An Unexpected Journey (2012) and The Hobbit: The Desolation of Smaug (2013).

Joe Gannon who takes on Associate Producer responsibilities in season ten, will be promoted to Producer in seasons eleven and twelve, then will serve as executive producer in the final season as well as sharing story editor duties in seasons twelve and thirteen. Gannon was of Irish descent and came to America when he was 17, accepting a job at the now defunct Avalon Ballroom in San Francisco. He ran light shows for the band Pink Floyd before becoming a producer. Archie Bunker's Place was his first major production credit and he also directed fifteen episodes of the series during its run. Gannon also created the spinoff series Gloria when Sally Struthers expressed a desire to return to episodic television in 1982. He would continue working with O'Connor as a producer on the series In the Heat of the Night. Most recently he has written episodes for the Law and Order franchise. Richard Baer comes on board in season ten as Story Editor along with Bill Larkin and Jerry Ross. Baer's writing credits included everything from the Jackie Cooper sitcom Hennesey to The Munsters, Love On a Rooftop, F Troop, Bewitched, and That Girl. Bill Larkin was a writer for many of Bob Hope's specials, and most recently was a writer for Donny and Marie's variety show. Larkin's sole credit after Archie Bunker's Place was as story editor on the short lived 1984 sitcom Spencer. Jerry Ross had written for Sanford and Son, Barney Miller, and Chico and the Man. He would move into a producer's role in the 1980s including work on Small Wonder and the Cosby Show.

In season eleven, the show had no less than seven Story Editors including Harriett Weiss and Patt Shea who penned three episodes in season nine and would remain on staff as writers. Shea and Weiss would co-create Gloria (along with Joe Gannon) in 1982. In addition to Story Editor responsibilities, Alan Rosen and Fred Rubin also write and produce episodes. After Archie Bunker's Place was cancelled in 1983, Rosen would produce episodes of Head of the Class while Rubin produced such sitcoms as Night Court, Family Matters, and Step by Step. Mark

Fink and Stephen Miller join in season eleven as well to edit stories and will also contribute to writing several scripts. Fink also worked on the series' Saved by the Bell, Who's the Boss?, and Full House while Miller continued writing on such shows as Simon and Simon, Magnum P.I., and Evening Shade. They both will assume producer responsibilities in season thirteen.

Always a vocal proponent for the character of Archie Bunker, Carroll O'Connor becomes story editor in season eleven, will write three scripts, and direct seven episodes.

Unlike All in the Family during its run, Archie Bunker's Place never benefitted from a consistent director. Among others, directors such as Peter Bonerz (The Bob Newhart Show), Dick Martin (half of the comedy team of Rowan and Martin), and Linda Day (who would go on to direct episodes of Kate & Allie, Married With Children, and Mad About You), all took turns in the director's chair. Gary Shimokawa, who served as associate director on over sixty episodes of All in the Family dating back to season four, is the series most frequent director with twenty-five episodes to his credit. While not uncommon for sitcoms to have multiple directors, it is this schizophrenic approach behind the camera which disassociates these final seasons from the rest of the body of work and reinforces how important the collaborative effort played a part in the success of the original series.

Supporting players such as Jason Wingreen, Allan Melvin, and Bill Quinn are elevated to feature character status and appear in the opening credits of the show. As the aging series wore on, many episodes focus on these characters. Problem is that, as a viewer, these characters work best in Archie's world as support to give him something to play off of. With few exceptions, the episodes which focus on these characters are not all that interesting as we do not have the emotional investment in them as we once did with the cast of All in the Family.

The wisest addition to the cast is that of legendary stage and film actor Martin Balsam. He was a veteran of the famed Actor's Studio and turned in fine dramatic performances in such films as On the Waterfront (1954), 12 Angry Men (1957), Psycho (1960), Breakfast at Tiffany's (1961), Seven Days in May and The Carpetbaggers (both 1964) and A Thousand Clowns (1965). Balsam and O'Connor had previously performed together in a 1960 teleplay "The Sacco-Vanzetti Story" which was a part of the NBC Sunday Showcase series.

Balsam lends an aura of class to the series and while a little unsteady at first, he and Carroll O'Connor develop a fine rapport.

His character of Murray Klein is introduced in the one-hour season ten opener **Archie's New Partner**. When Archie wants to knock out an adjoining wall and expand to the restaurant next door, Harry refuses and sells his share of the bar. Enter Murray Klein who is ready to buy Harry out. Klein is not only Jewish but an ex-boxer who does not take kindly to Archie's anti-Semitic remarks and where as many shouted Archie down in the past, one gets the feeling that Murray would just as soon beat the hell out of Archie. On the verge of giving up and backing out of the deal, it is not until the final moments of the episode which take place in the office at Archie's Place where Murray talks with Stephanie and realizes that she is Jewish. Not only has Archie bought her a Star of David necklace, he has joined her temple. Having a change of heart, Murray decides to give the relationship some time to grow as the camera closes in on the top of a desk where both of their hats lay side by side as the episode fades out.

Anne Meara joins the cast in the episode **Hiring the Cook** but there is a catch, her homosexual nephew Fred comes with the deal as a waiter. Fred (played by Dino Scofield) would only last five episodes at Archie Bunker's Place. According to an interview with the Archive of American Television, Meara was recommended for the role by producer Mort Lachman and had been friends with Carroll O'Connor since they performed together in a stage production of Ulysses in Nighttown. Along with her husband Jerry Stiller, Meara was an alum of Second City and her and Stiller branched out together as a team. Stiller and Meara were staples of television variety shows in the 1960s and they are parents to comedian-actor Ben Stiller. Meara plays Irish-Catholic cook Veronica Rooney who has no qualms about putting Archie in his place upon their first meeting together. She is a tough character but shows a humor and vulnerability which keeps her relationship with Archie on a more believable level. Jerry Stiller shows up as her ex-husband Carmine in season ten's **Veronica's Ex** and the season twelve-episode **Relapse** which would also be Meara's last for the series. With the restaurant now built and added to the set, more kitchen help was needed. Originally billed simply as "Puerto Rican", Abraham Alvarez was brought on as Jose the cook. Alvarez had appeared on such shows as Wonder Woman and Emergency and more recently acted in episodes of Law & Order and Louie. Joe Rosario would be added to the cast in season eleven as Raoul. Rosario's last known credit was a guest spot on Scarecrow and Mrs. King in 1987. An order window with a door that raises up and down is installed behind the bar which oversees the kitchen. The door serves several purposes. Instead of closing cases as he has done so many times in the past, Archie can simply shut the window and therefore shut them out. It also acts very much like the joke wall from Laugh-In as Veronica, Jose, and Manuel open and close the window to punctuate various scenes with wisecracks or one-liners like Statler and Waldorf in the balcony on the Muppet Show.

Mike and Gloria return in the one-hour **Thanksgiving Reunion**. Things were a little tentative yet hopeful when we last saw the Stivic's in the season nine-episode **California, Here We Are** and while their marriage has survived, no holiday would be complete for the Bunker's without some type of crisis. Here we learn that Mike has lost his job, not because of the state of unemployment in the country as Archie originally assumes, but because he was fired for protesting in the nude over the construction of a nuclear power plant near a nude beach. If that is not bad enough, Archie learns that Gloria had joined him as well. Compared to the rest of the season, this episode is a stand out. Archie is a little more engaged in the dialog and a lot of the traditional series' elements are present; saying grace at the table and arguing about a hot button topic of the day – in this instance nuclear energy. Yet when compared to the characters that we watched on All in the Family, the confrontation lacks the bite we have come to expect. While it is great to see these characters again, the results feel a little out of step and old fashioned as if Mike and Gloria no longer belong in the world that the series now finds itself in.

In **Archie and the Oldest Profession**, we are introduced to Dotty Wertz, a prostitute who uses Archie's Place as a hookup for clients. Dotty is played by Sheree North who is best known to Jerry Lewis fans as the woman he dances the jitterbug with in the 1954 Martin and Lewis film Living It Up. Her character is given a bit of a story arc later in the season in the episode **Barney and the Hooker.** The character of Barney is usually played as bit of a buffoon however in this episode, he falls in love with Dottie and asks her to marry him. Allan Melvin turns in a very sympathetic performance and their relationship is very genuine. Unfortunately, aside from a cursory mention in a few subsequent episodes, Dottie is never seen from again which is surprising as Sheree North was nominated for Outstanding Lead Actress in a Comedy Series at the 1980 Emmy Awards. Soon enough, Barney is back to acting the fool. This episode is one of those exceptions to the rule about the supporting cast as the viewer is invested in Barney's feelings. It is a shame that this story line never developed and allowed Melvin to spread his wings and add more dimension to his character especially since he was now a featured player on the series.

In **Man of the Year**, some con artists throw a high school reunion at Archie's Place naming him Man of the Year. Although Archie sees them sneak out before splitting the profits of the nights take, he talks Murray out of calling the police as for the first time in his life he feels important and does not want to spoil everyone else's evening. Archie tells Murray that his father never felt he would amount to anything and would hit him with a shovel. "Mine laughed" replies Murray. It is the first moment where the two men find something to bond over.

Murray has been avoiding introducing his new girlfriend to his mother since she's not Jewish yet unknowingly, Edith invites them all over in **The Shabbat Dinner**. The story is a somewhat reworking of the season four-episode **Lionel's Engagement** where the Jeffersons disapprove of Lionel's choice of a partner. It is Jean Stapleton's final appearance in the series and takes Murray's Mother into the kitchen to talk with her saying that his mother should not let Murray's happiness make her miserable. For Edith, the kitchen table has always been a source of wisdom for her much the same as Archie's chair has been for him. Although in his case, the wisdom has mostly been misguided.

If Archie Bunker's Place exists for anything, it is for the one-hour season eleven premiere **Archie Alone**. Feeling Edith's character had said all she needed to say, Jean Stapleton announced she would not return when production resumed for the season. With an off-camera wife most of the time, it limited the stories that could be told for Archie so the decision was made to kill Edith off. It would expand the narrative for Archie Bunker plus it provided the series with its finest moment in its final years. In an interview with the Archive of American Television, Stapleton related a story in which she received a call from Norman Lear about killing Edith's character. Lear was final holdout with the production and network team to greenlight this direction for the series. Stapleton reminded Lear that "(Edith) is only fiction." After a long pause, Lear replied "To me, she isn't."⁵³ It's a very telling and bittersweet anecdote as to just how much the series and its characters meant to him. Lear was not the only one with such strong emotions. The night the episode aired; Stapleton was in Winston-Salem attending the opening of a theatre. The next morning when the hotel maid came in to the room, she saw Jean and screamed "I thought you were dead!" It is a tribute to the reality of the Edith character and how connected and ingrained she was in the public conscious. It Is understandable why Stapleton wanted to move on to other opportunities.

In the episode, some weeks have passed since Edith has passed away (from a stroke in her sleep) and while Archie is struggling inside, he is doing all he can to put on a brave face reassuring neighbors and friends that he and Stephanie are doing great. He refuses to sign Edith's death benefit when the life insurance man comes to the bar - and mistakenly calls her Judith due to a typo on the paperwork. He has not slept in their bed since her death, choosing to sleep on the couch downstairs and has not cleaned her things out of their bedroom. Trying to be the strong support for Stephanie, he changes the subject whenever she wants to talk. When it is discovered that Stephanie has been cutting class because of her grieving, the school counselor calls Archie in. She says she believes he is wrong for avoiding discussing it with

Stephanie and if he does not, it could have damaging consequences for her as she matures. An angry Archie leaves to find support in his friends. He asks Murray over for dinner so that he can talk with Stephanie and find out what is wrong. During his conversation, Murray relates that after his father died, he did not start feeling better until he talked with people about it. Stephanie explains that she wants to talk but Archie changes the subject. He will not answer the phone or open any of the cards that have been sent to the house. Murray finds out what Stephanie's problem is; it is Archie. The emotional distance Archie has put between this event and those around him who love him most becomes claustrophobic.

With his grief closing in on him he has no other choice but to finally face the fact that Edith is gone. Archie asks Veronica and his neighbor Polly to come by and clean the bedroom out. Taking the advice of her school counselor, Stephanie finds a pin to keep in memory of Edith. Once Veronica and Polly leave, Archie finally feels brave enough to enter the room again. Finding a slipper under the bed, he takes a seat and clutches the slipper. Archie can no longer avoid dealing with it and says "You had no right to leave me that way Edith without giving me just one more chance to say I love you" and finally breaks down. The guilt he has felt is perfectly conveyed in this very moment. He could not allow Stephanie or anyone else to grieve as he himself has not grieved and said goodbye. Stephanie walks in on him during this moment and he is now able to articulate his pain and comforts her. The scene is perfect and plays so much better than a traditional death scene would have played. Very much like the maid at the hotel that Jean Stapleton mentioned, we as viewers have memories of Edith so we are not afraid to emotionally invest in this moment and take this journey with Archie as his monolog unfolds. Like Archie, we grieve and we cry. It is an incredibly moving moment and the last of such moments for the remainder of the series. When viewed today, it still holds its emotional impact. Not surprisingly, O'Connor received a Peabody Award for his performance in this episode.

This is a pivotal moment for the series. With Archie now on the road to healing and having to raise Stephanie by himself, future storylines will explore life after Edith. These stories will give the character his strongest moments in these final seasons.

In **Alone Again**, Archie considers moving to a condo as everything in the house reminds him of Edith. Archie struggles a bit with the decision and while looking a property over, Mr. Van Ranseleer reminds him that "the pain will lessen and the memories will grow sweeter." When his house is being shown to an enterprising young couple who is eager to gut it and update the home, he changes his mind. Like changing his mind about selling his chair, he realizes that the memories will indeed grow sweeter with time. In **Hiring the Housekeeper**, Archie decides he needs someone to stay with Stephanie while he is at work. Polly's sister-in-law Ellen Canby is hired. Canby is played by actress Barbara Meek who, like many series' actors, came from the theatre. With no explanation, she will eventually disappear from the series after the season twelve-episode **Gloria Comes Home**. At first Archie's bigoted remarks are a little too much for her but after a discussion with Murray, she decides to give it a shot. Her and Archie form a bond and when he is seen shopping with her in **The Incident**, Archie punches out the President of his lodge after he levels a racial epithet about Mrs. Canby. Faced with being kicked out of the lodge, he writes an apology letter. When he learns that Mrs. Canby's brother was beaten to death simply for walking in the wrong neighborhood, Archie decides to tear up the letter and quit the lodge.

Although he now has help, raising Stephanie is a struggle for Archie. In **The Camping Trip**, Stephanie wants Archie to attend a father-daughter trip with him. He refuses at first saying he is worried that someone his age should not be called Dad, especially since Stephanie has already lost Edith. Yet, Archie does have a change of heart and agrees to attend the trip. In the two-part episode **Custody**, Stephanie's Grandmother (Estelle Harris) returns for a visit. Harris is played by Academy Award winning actress

Celeste Holm who won the statue in 1947's Gentleman's Agreement and was nominated again for the 1950 classic All About Eve. Grandma Harris wants Stephanie to come and live with her permanently as with Edith now gone, she feels Archie is not fit to be Stephanie's guardian. Archie already feels defeated as her grandmother can provide all the things that he cannot. While Grandma Harris argues that Stephanie may suffer from being raised by a man with such bigoted and prejudiced views, Archie counters that despite those things he raised a happy and healthy daughter in Gloria. When the time came, Gloria left the house under good circumstances. Gloria did not run away like Harris' daughter did when she married Floyd. In the end, the judge decides in Archie's favor as Stephanie has established roots and an emotional bond with him.

At the end of season eleven, Martin Balsam grew tired of playing the role stating he was "faintly uncomfortable with Murray Klein and the "ethnic irritation" that was supposed to develop"[54] and decided to leave the series so he could focus on returning to character acting. Recalled O'Connor "We went into the Murray Klein character without really knowing, but hoping something would emerge that would make him a dominant figure. It never did."[55] His departure changed the tone of the series and shook what was an already unstable foundation in the cast. His absence is felt through the remainder of the series. He will return for a guest shot in the season thirteen-episode **Store Wars**, one of the final episodes of the series.

With Balsam now gone, a new cast member was added at the beginning of season twelve. Eighteen-year-old Denise Miller was hired for the part of Archie's niece Billie Bunker. Billie is the daughter of Archie's brother Fred (one of the three other sisters Archie's niece Linda mentions in the season three-episode **Lionel Steps Out**). Miller co-starred with Abe Vigoda in the Barney Miller spin-off Fish as well as the short-lived disco-themed sitcom Makin' It before joining the cast. Billie will provide a conduit between Archie and Stephanie to help with the difficulties Stephanie faces as she enters her teenage years. She will also take on the role of the woman of the house in many ways as well. Miller's presence shines however it is a bit of stunt casting to try and draw in a younger audience for the increasingly ageing series. Yet prior to the start of the third season, TV Guide noted that the series "has now reached a point where it is absolutely fail-safe"[56] going further to quote now former series producer Mort Lachman who claimed "You couldn't kill it with a stick...there is no way to stop it."[57]

In the two-part episode **Growing Up is Hard to Do**, Stephanie has her bat mitzvah so Archie and Grandma Harris throw a party at Archie's house. Stephanie's father Floyd returns to join in Stephanie's celebration. The gang from the bar have given Stephanie a money tree. Floyd and Archie are at odds as her father has been absent most of her life but it is important to Stephanie that her father is with her on her day. As with previous visits, there is also an ulterior motive behind Floyd's visit. He wants money to invest in a business. He gives Stephanie a broach from her mother only it is a random piece of junk that he has found somewhere. When Grandma Harris refuses to financially assist Floyd, he makes his way up to Stephanie's bedroom where the money tree has been placed and proceeds to steal everything. Stephanie catches him and with her dreams of a relationship with her father shattered, she makes her first adult decision and tells him to take all the money and leave. When Archie comes up to the room, he notices the money and Floyd are gone. He begins to rant about Floyd and Stephanie's decision but all she wants is comfort and embraces Archie. In a nicely framed scene, we see the bare money tree in the foreground with Archie holding Stephanie in the background. Grandma Harris arrives in the room to console her. In the end, so she has something to believe in, Stephanie wants to know if at least the broach really belonged to her mother. Not wanting to destroy possibly the last positive thought Stephanie might have about her father, Grandma Harris lies and tells her yes.

Archie starts to date again and in the episode **Three's a Crowd**, he falls for Katherine Logan, a woman who is matched with Barney through a dating service. Initially he struggles as, although Edith is dead, he still has not let her go in his heart. Katherine is played by character actress Yvonne Wilder who may be best known for her role in the 1961 musical West Side Story (trivia note: one of the episodes she appears in is titled **West Side Astoria**). As Archie heals, he sees more of her and the relationship is quite sweet although it is hard for us, the viewer, to imagine him with anyone else but Edith. The character of Katherine Logan will return in three additional episodes culminating in a dinner with Katherine's family in **The Battle of Bunker III**, where Archie learns that Katherine is part Hispanic and goes about offending her entire family. To stay with her, Katherine demands that Archie must change. However, by the end of the season she will be gone with only a quick explanation as to her absence in the beginning of the final season.

Harry's Investment is noteworthy for the first appearance of Barry Gordon as Gary Rabinowitz. Gary's role will grow as he becomes the love interest for Billie. Gordon will be added to the cast in the final season. The 33-year-old Gordon was already a TV veteran with guest spots on such sitcoms as Make Room for Daddy and Leave it Beaver as well as feature film appearances in the 1960 Jerry Lewis comedy Cinderfella and A Thousand Clowns (1965). Gordon and Denise Miller were no strangers as they co-starred together in the Barney Miller spin-off Fish.

In one of the more solid episodes **Sex and the Single Parent**, Stephanie brings a slip home for Archie to sign so she can attend sex education classes. Archie refuses and joins a group of concerned parents led by Ronald Scott (played by Alan Fudge) to speak out about having this class taught in school. When Archie eavesdrops on a conversation between Billie, Stephanie, and Ronald's daughter Martha in which he finds out Martha is pregnant, he has a change of heart. He realizes that could be Stephanie and perhaps he does not have all the answers to guide her through this time in her life. As Ronald comes by to pick up his daughter, Archie back peddles on his stance "We're talking about the children!" Ronald argues, trying to convince Archie to move forward. Archie agrees as he gently puts his hand on Martha's face. TV Guide noted that this episode "was an excellent opportunity for parents to broach the subject of sex with their children."[58]

Sally Struthers returns to the series in the one-hour episode **Gloria Comes Home**. While not explained, Mike apparently found a new job then left it, Gloria, and Joey to join a commune. It is a contrived storyline indicative of situation comedies where an event is hastily and sometimes sloppily explained so a plot can move forward. Perhaps without the participation of Rob Reiner in a storyline, this was the only way to handle that Gloria is now alone but it feels like a bit of a cheat. Archie wants Gloria and Joey to stay with him however Gloria wants to try and make it on her own. A spin-off series was developed by Joe Gannon, Harriett Weiss, and Pat Shea where Gloria would move to Fox Ridge New York to work for a veterinarian. The vet was played by Burgess Meredith who was friends with Carroll O'Connor since he directed him in the 1958 off-Broadway play Ulysses in Nighttown. Meredith is probably best known on the small screen for his portrayal of the Penguin in the 1960s hit series Batman as well as several appearances in the anthology series The Twilight Zone. Meredith also acted in such films as Of Mice and Men (1939) and the first three installments of the Rocky franchise in addition to a memorable turn in the comedy Grumpy Old Men (1993) and its sequel. A pilot was directed by All in the Family veteran Paul Bogart which featured Archie dropping Gloria off for her first day of work. When the series was picked up, production was moved from Television City over to Universal and a new pilot was taped. This essentially cut out the original production staff to guide and further develop the series. Although it performed somewhat respectably in the ratings when it premiered following Archie Bunker's Place in the Fall of 1982 and finished the season at #18, the series was cancelled after 20 episodes.

The final season has few bright spots. Archie's Brother returns once again in **Father Christmas** but Billie wants nothing to do with him because as a child, he did not want her in his life. When we first hear about Archie's brother in **Lionel Steps Out** from season three, he is described as an evolved Father with no suggested problems holding down a wife or loving his four daughters. As the story is recalled, it turns out that her mother was the one who decided to leave and did not want Billie.

In **The Red Herring**, Archie questions his friendship with Mr. Van Rensellar when he finds out he was called to the HUAC during the cold war. **I Can Manage** tells the story of Archie falling for a woman who is heading up a conference for bar and restaurant owners on how to improve business. He winds up spending the night with her only to find out in the morning that she is still married. Archie suspects Billie is smoking marijuana in **Bunker Madness** only it is really Stephanie and her friends. Archie kicks Billie out of the house and by the end of the episode after all is revealed, Stephanie pleads with Archie that she really wishes Billie would not move out. Archie reconciles with Billie who in turn tells Stephanie that she'd better start thinking of herself and not go along with what everyone else does. Though it does not have the label of 'a very special episode' and although it is well acted and executed, such a storyline would be more comfortable as an episode of Facts of Life or Growing Pains. It does not belong in the world of Archie Bunker.

Gary and Billie's relationship comes to an end in **No One Said it Was Easy** and Archie is there to comfort Billie and help her pick up the pieces. On April 4, 1983, Gary and Billie talk about life after their breakup in **I'm Torn Here**, the final episode of season thirteen and what would turn out to be the final episode of the series. The show that was once a ratings powerhouse, limped across the finish line with its main character nowhere to be found in the final moments of the episode.

For what was described as a "fail safe" show not two years earlier, a little over a month after the final episode of season thirteen aired, Tom Shales reported in the Washington Post that "Archie Bunker died yesterday. Or rather, CBS decided to pull the plug on the life-support systems that have kept him alive for the past three years."[59] The article continues stating "Associates of (Norman) Lear say he would have preferred it if Archie had expired when "Family" ended its run in 1979 but O'Connor and CBS wanted to keep Archie alive"[60] CBS Entertainment president B. Donald Grant was more specific,"(the show) was canceled because "all good things have to come to an end. 'M*A*S*H' did. 'Mary Tyler Moore' did. It was time."[61]

Archie Bunker's Place focused too much on its supporting cast, especially in its final two seasons. The strongest of the series episodes feature Archie although he has little in common with his established character and is played more like a mumbling curmudgeon, a trait that started to creep in during the last third of All in the Family's run. Archie Bunker eventually becomes a supporting player in the series that features his name in the title. The storylines of the supporting characters, would feel more at home on another series. In Archie Bunker's Place we do not feel as connected to them as we did Edith, Mike, and Gloria. Many times, Archie is reduced to providing commentary to the action around him as opposed to being a catalyst or a part of the action itself. "The Bunker character lost much of its bite, even a great deal of bark."[62] wrote Tom Shales in the Washington Post.

O'Connor who was pulling down a reported $100,000 a week by this time, did not expect the series to end here so it is hard to envision what a fourteenth season would have looked like or if a proper finale would have been developed. The show came to two proper conclusions in both seasons 8 and 9 so it was left to be that two late series additions would be the last images tied to the series that the viewer would see. Without the fanfare that was afforded a show like M*A*S*H for its finale, Archie Bunker's Place ended with a phone call to O'Connor informing him that the network would not be bringing it back for another year. It was just as well; the show had long since run its course. Of the remaining Lear shows, One Day at a Time was cancelled the following season, and in July of 1985 the final episode of The Jeffersons would air which brought to the end an era that changed the face of television forever.

When All in the Family premiered in 1971 it was a breath of fresh air amidst a schedule of aging sitcoms. Similarly, by 1983 Archie Bunker's Place *was* the aging sitcom. The landscape of television was changing once again. Prime time soap operas and action shows were in vogue as viewers turned their loyalties to Dallas, Dynasty, Falcon Crest, Magnum P.I., and The A-Team. O'Connor felt betrayed by the network as shows which preformed behind his in the ratings received a renewal. Danielle Brisebois was more pointed in her recollections saying that they should have shown more respect for the series by giving it a proper finale. However, looking back to the end of season eight that respectful finale already occurred. Performing well enough in the ratings and with the desire on the part of its star to continue with the allure of having more overall control over production, the series moved forward. Archie Bunker's Place still connected and performed well enough to remain in the top 20 until its final season but in retrospect, it had too much working against it.

Although Archie Bunker's Place had five Emmy nominations over its four years, it was never recognized with a win by the Academy and not once was Carroll O'Connor nominated during this time. The Young Artists

Awards, established in the late 70's, acknowledged Danielle Brisebois for her work on the series during all four years, giving her a win in 1982. The 94 episodes that followed season nine did little to further the legacy of the original series which is why Archie Bunker's Place plays just fine on its own in syndication. While there are some connections which feel familiar to the viewer, it is a series which is difficult to embrace and hard to defend. There no longer was a place for Archie Bunker in the 1980s; he was finally dummied up.

season ten episodes

Archie's New Partner (one hour) 9-23-79
When Archie makes plans to expand the bar to the restaurant next door, Harry sells his piece of the bar to a new partner – Murray Klein.

Episode notes
- Originally aired in a one-hour timeslot, this is split into two episodes in syndication and on DVD (with some minor edits) in both Archie Bunker's Place – the Complete First Season (Sony 2006) and as a bonus feature in All in the Family – the Complete Series (Shout! Factory 2012)
- Archie took the original loan on the bar for $20,000 in October of 1977 (**Archie Gets the Business**). By September of 1979, he owes $19,724.50.

- Jay Gerber plays the attorney Levy. Gerber previously appeared as Stretch Cunningham's brother in the season seven-episode **Stretch Cunningham, Goodbye**.
- Norma Donaldson returns as the loan officer Ms. Watson. She can also be seen in the season eight premiere **Archie Gets the Business** and will return in season ten in **The Cook**.
- Danny Dayton appears as Hank Pivnik.
- This is the first appearance for Connie Sawyer as Murray's Mother Rose.
- Florence Halop makes the first of two appearances as Aunt Gussie. She may be best known for her role as Florence Kleiner on the series Night Court. She is the sister of All in the Family alum Billy Halop.

Edith Gets Hired 9-30-79

Edith applies for a new job at the Rego Park Center and worries her termination from the Sunshine Home will affect her new job.

Episode notes
- Jean Stapleton appears in this episode.
- Edith's hours are Monday through Friday Noon to 8pm and she is paid $5 an hour, a $2.35 raise from her last stated income at the Sunshine Home in the season nine-episode **Edith Versus the Bank**.

- Iconic character actor William Schallert plays Dr. Wakeford. Schallert has close to 400 roles to his credit at the time of his passing in May of 2016, his last appearance being in the CBS sitcom 2 Broke Girls. The versatile and reliable actor lent his talents to numerous television shows and movies including Leave it to Beaver, The Many Loves of Dobie Gillis, the series The Patty Duke Show, a recurring role as Admiral Hargrade on Get Smart, Simon and Simon, Rosanne, How I Met Your Mother, and Desperate Housewives in a career that spanned almost 70 years.

Archie and the Oldest Profession 10-2-79
Archie and Murray must ask a prostitute to stop arranging for business at Archie's Place.

Episode notes
- The part of Dotty Wertz is played by Sheree North and will return this season in the episode **Barney and the Hooker.** North had a lengthy career dating back to the early 1950s and can be seen as the jitterbug dancer with partner Jerry Lewis in the Martin and Lewis film Living it Up (1954) as well as numerous appearances on television including Burke's Law, The Fugitive, Alias Smith and Jones, The Golden Girls, and Seinfeld.

Edith Versus the Energy Crisis 10-14-79

Archie must tighten up and conserve energy.

Episode notes

- Jean Stapleton appears in this episode.
- While it has been missing in previous episodes, the picture of Mike and Gloria can be seen again on the ledge in the living room.

Bosom Partners 10-21-79

Archie tries (unsuccessfully) to buy Murray out.

Episode notes

- This is the first episode of the series to be co-directed by Carroll O'Connor.

Building the Restaurant 10-28-79

With funds running low, everybody pitches in to build the restaurant.

Episode notes

- Film and television actor Jack Carter plays Louie the Loanshark. Carter appeared on such shows as Ben Casey, Batman, CHiPs, Parks and Recreation, and Shameless and was a staple of game shows in the 1970's and 80s. Carter passed away on June 28, 2015
- Ron Feinberg appears as the building contractor Swenson. He appeared in episodes of It Takes a

Thief, Here Come the Brides, The Partridge Family, and Mary Hartman, Mary Hartman. In addition, he provided voices for many animated series including Jana of the Jungle, Alvin & the Chipmunks, and The Transformers.

- Abraham Alvarez makes his first appearance in the series. Billed as Manuel – one of Swensen's helpers – he will return to the series in a recurring role as Jose' the cook.
- Danny Dayton appears as Hank Pivnik.
- Andy Garcia appears as Hay-Soos, another helper for Swensen. Garcia would go on to a successful motion picture career in such films as The Godfather: Part III (1990) and When a Man Loves a Woman (1994). He has also guested on episodes of the HBO series Ballers.

The Cook 11-4-79
Archie hires Veronica Rooney and her gay nephew Fred to work at Archie's Place.

Episode notes
- This is the first appearance for Anne Meara as Veronica and her name is added to the opening credits.
- This is the final appearance of Norma Donaldson as the loan officer Ms. Watson.

- Abraham Alvarez appears in this episode however he is listed simply as "Puerto Rican" in the closing credits.
- Dean Scofield (billed as Dino Scofield) makes the first of five appearances as Fred.
- Danny Dayton appears as Hank Pivnik.

Murray and the Liquor Board 11-11-79
A conviction from Murray's past could threaten the renewal of the liquor license at Archie's Place.

Episode notes
- Danny Dayton appears as Hank Pivnik.

Thanksgiving Reunion (one hour) 11-18-79
Mike and Gloria return to Hauser Street to celebrate Thanksgiving.

Episode notes
- Jean Stapleton, Rob Reiner, and Sally Struthers appear in this episode.
- When Archie tells Joey he is not getting a dollar, if you look you can see the boom microphone in frame.
- This episode makes references to the season seven-episodes **Gloria's False Alarm** and **The Draft Dodger**.

- While originally aired in a one-hour timeslot, this episode is split into two parts in syndication and on the 2006 DVD release from Sony.

Barney and the Hooker 11-25-79
Barney begins to date Dottie.

Episode notes
- Barney's divorce from Blanche is final in this episode.
- This is the second and final appearance of Sheree North as Dottie Wertz.
- This is the first episode where Abraham Alvarez is billed as Jose.
- Dino Scofield makes his second appearance as Fred.

Man of the Year 12-2-79
A con-artist couple talk Archie into holding a class reunion at the bar where Archie is named man of the year.

Episode notes
- If you look at the yearbook that Phil Weber thumbs through, you will see that all the pages are blank.
- In this episode, Archie says he went to Bryant High School in Long Island City and Edith went to Bayside. While the schools have not been named up to now, it was originally suggested in the season three-episode **Class Reunion** that Edith went to a

different high school. This was contradicted in the season seven-episode **Archie's Secret Passion** where it is discussed that they went to the same school together.

- Dino Scofield appears as Fred.

The Shabbat Dinner 12-9-79
Murray brings his new girlfriend to a Jewish dinner that Edith has cooked only to be confronted by his mother.

Episode notes
- This is the final appearance of Jean Stapleton as Edith Bunker.
- This is the second and final appearance for Connie Sawyer as Murray's Mother Rose. While her character will pass away (offscreen) in the season twelve-episode **Death of a Saint**, in real life Sawyer lived to 105! One of her final appearances was in the Showtime series Ray Donovan. She died on January 21, 2018
- Florence Halop makes her final appearance as Aunt Gussie.

Barney's Lawsuit 12-16-79
Barney sues Archie's Place when he falls off a barstool.

Episode notes

- Barney mentions being engaged to Dottie. He will soon be dating again with no explanation as to what happened between the two of them.
- Danny Dayton appears as Hank Pivnik.

Blanche and Murray 12-30-79

Murray begins dating Barney's ex-wife Blanche.

Episode notes

- Estelle Parsons makes her final appearance in the series as Blanche.
- While in the previous episode, Barney mentions being engaged to Dottie, in this episode he says they are only dating indicating perhaps that the episodes were produced in a different order than which they aired.

Murray's Daughter 1-6-80

Murray's daughter surprises him with a visit after being estranged for six years.

Episode notes

- This is the first episode written by Carroll O'Connor
- Murray's daughter is played by Talia Balsam who is the real-life daughter of actor Martin Balsam. She appeared on Hill Street Blues, Family Ties, two episodes of Murder, She Wrote and most recently appeared in the HBO series Divorce and co-starred

in the AMC series Mad Men with real life husband John Slattery. She was previously married to actor George Clooney.

The Ambush 1-27-80

With a rash of robberies happening in the neighborhood, Archie and Murray guard the bar and are held up by two women.

Episode notes

- Danny Dayton appears as Hank Pivnik.

The Return of Sammy 2-3-79

After seeing Sammy Davis Jr. on a talk show, Archie invites him down to the bar for a reunion.

Episode notes

- We learn the address of Archie's Place in this episode is 5219 Northern Boulevard in Queens.
- Sammy Davis Jr. guest stars in this episode.
- Dino Scofield makes his fourth appearance as Fred.
- Mel Bryant appears as 'man' in this episode. He will be featured in three further episodes of the series.
- Danny Dayton appears as Hank Pivnik.

Archie Fixes Up Fred 2-10-80

Feeling pressure from his lodge brother Tom to keep the bar decent, Archie tries to convert Fred by fixing him up with the laundry service girl Linda. Spoiler alert – Tom is gay too.

Episode notes

- Jack Dodson appears as Tom and is best known as Howard Sprague in the classic sitcom The Andy Griffith Show and its spinoff Mayberry R.F.D. Dodson also appeared on various television series including the part of Ralph Malph's father Mickey on Happy Days, Barney Miller, St. Elsewhere, and Growing Pains. He reprised his role of Howard Sprague in an episode of It's Garry Shandling's Show.
- This is the final appearance for Dino Schofield in the role of Fred. Although Fred and Veronica came as a package deal when they were hired at Archie's Place, that loyalty has been forgotten as Veronica will stay on as the cook.
- Mel Bryant makes his second appearance in the series, this time playing "George".
- Heidi Hagman plays the role of Linda from the laundry service. Archie will hire her as a waitress in the following season and she will appear in an additional four episodes before disappearing from the show. She is the daughter of Larry Hagman and her short career resume includes some guest spots on Dallas.

Father and Daughter Night 2-17-80

Archie and Murray both perform with Stephanie for her talent show.

Episode notes
- Danny Dayton appears as Hank Pivnik.

Van Ranseleer's Operation 3-2-80
The gang raises money to pay for an experimental operation which may restore Mr. Van Ranseleer's sight.

Veronica's Ex 3-9-80
Veronica's ex-husband Carmine returns for a visit.

Episode notes
- Real life husband Jerry Stiller plays Carmine. He will reprise the role later in the season twelve-episode **Relapse**.
- Danny Dayton appears as Hank Pivnik.

A Small Mafia Favor 3-23-80
Visited by an old friend who is now a mafia kingpin, Murray unknowingly sets up a hit for rival mob boss's murder.

Episode notes
- Mel Bryant returns for his third appearance in the series. For this role, he has been promoted to a Detective investigating the murder.
- Danny Dayton makes his final appearance as Hank Pivnik
- Vinnie Mulvaney is played by John McLiam. McLiam can also be seen in the Woody Allen comedy

Sleeper (1973), in addition to nearly 170 other film and television credits.

- This was one of the final acting credits for actor Michael Strong (Tony Bremmer). Strong had almost 100 appearances to his credit, mostly in television, including The Defenders, The Fugitive, Star Trek, I Spy, The Green Hornet, and The Streets of San Francisco.

season eleven episodes

Archie Alone (one hour) 11-2-80

Archie tries to cope and move forward after the death of Edith

Episode notes

- Edith is buried at Meadow Glen Cemetery.
- Edith's clothes are donated to the Sunshine Home.
- This is the second appearance of Janet MacLachlan as Polly.
- This episode is co-directed by Carroll O'Connor (along with longtime Associate Director Gary Shimokowa)
- We learn in this episode that Barney has been a bridge inspector for 28 years.
- Heidi Hagman appears as Linda
- Renne Jarrett makes her first of two appearances as Stephanie's counselor Mrs. Kathy Wakefield. She

will appear again later this season in **Stephanie's Science Project**. Ironically, she appeared in two other television shows where the last name of her character was Wakefield. Jarrett can also be seen in Barnaby Jones, Mod Squad, and The Streets of San Francisco. Her last known screen credit was in a 1985 episode of Hotel.

- Jason Wingreen and Bill Quinn are added to the opening credits of the series in this episode.

Home Again 11-9-80
Struggling with the memories of Edith around the house, Archie considers selling 704 Hauser St. and moving into a condo.

Episode notes
- Archie believes he can about $62/$63,000 for his house. In the season two episode **The Blockbuster** which aired eight years earlier, he is offered $35,000. He originally paid $14,000 for his home.
- Heidi Hagman makes her third appearance as Linda.

Hiring the Housekeeper 11-16-80
With Edith now gone and his schedule at the bar somewhat demanding, Archie hires a housekeeper.

Episode notes

- This is the first appearance of Barbara Meek as Ellen Canby.
- This is the third and final appearance for Janet MacLachlan as Polly. She died on October 11, 2010
- This is the fourth and final series appearance for Mel Bryant. Here he portrays Detective Ed Swanson again (as he did in the season ten finale **A Small Mafia Favor**) and we find out in this episode he is married to Archie's neighbor Polly. The role of her husband was originally portrayed by Richard Ward in the season nine-episode **The Family Next Door** and although his first name was Ed, their last name was originally Lewis.

The Wildcat Strike 11-23-80

A new waitress at Archie's Place forces the staff to Unionize.

Episode notes

- The part of Samantha is played by Lane Binkley who also appears in such shows as Family, Eight is Enough, and David Cassidy – Man Undercover.
- Heidi Hagman appears as Linda.
- This is the first appearance of semi-series regular Joe Rosario as Raoul.

Veronica and the Health Inspector 11-30-80

Veronica falls for the health inspector who is less than half her age.

Episode notes

- Steve Connery is played by Paul Sylvan. Sylvan can also be seen in episodes of Police Story, CPO Sharkey, and Charlie's Angels.
- This is the final appearance for Heidi Hagman as Linda.

Murrays' Wife 12-7-80

When Murray's wife returns for a visit, their relationship is rejuvenated until he finds out she has plans to revamp Archie's Place and get rid of everyone.

Episode notes

- Shelley is played by actress Carol Eve Rossen. Rossen also appeared in episodes of The Fugitive, Vega$, The Streets of San Francisco, Barney Miller, and Law & Order.

The Camping Trip 12-14-80

Archie struggles with the decision to take Stephanie on a camping trip with her girl's club.

Episode notes

- This is the first of six episodes for Mark Lonow as Barry Bloom. Prior to this episode he has only been referenced off camera. Lonow previously appeared as Mike's friend Peter Gavaris in the season seven-episode **Mike Goes Skiing** and appeared in many series during the 70's and 80's including David Cassidy – Man Undercover, Fantasy Island, Hill Street Blues, Webster, and Murphy Brown.

The Incident 12-21-80
While shopping with Mrs. Canby, Archie knocks out his lodge President after he uses a racial epithet.

Episode notes
- Gordy Bruns is played by Pat McNamara. McNamara can also be seen in episodes of M*A*S*H, Family Ties, Law & Order, and NYPD Blue. He has also appeared in feature films such as Silence of the Lambs (1991).
- Barbara Meek is added to the opening credits in this episode.

Custody pt. 1 1-4-81
Custody pt. 2 1-11-81
With Edith now gone, Stephanie's Grandma Harris resurfaces and wants Stephanie to live with her.

Episode notes
- This is the first of three appearances for Academy Award winner Celeste Holm as Grandma Estelle Harris. Holm's career began in Hollywood in the

mid-40s in such films as Gentleman's Agreement (for which she won the Academy Award) in 1947 and All About Eve in 1950 (for which she was nominated). She transitioned to television in the 1950s playing the title role in the short-lived series Honestly, Celeste! in 1954 and went on to appear in such shows as Dr. Kildare, Burke's Law, Falcon Crest, Touched By an Angel, and The Beat.

- Although this episode aired after the New Year, it is centered around Christmas and Barney mentions it is his third Christmas alone.

- Archie refers to paying for Stephanie's operation in the season nine episode **The Appendectomy**

- Archie mentions that the last time they saw Floyd, he gave him $200 yet in that season nine-episode (**The Return of Stephanie's Father**) Archie only gives him $100.

- Archie re-enacts one of his pantomime suicides in part I of this story when Stephanie is describing all the things she needs to buy.

- Judge McGuire is played by Lloyd Nolan whose career went back to the mid-30s where he co-starred with James Cagney in G-Men (1935). He appeared in 160 roles during his career. His last appearance was in the 1986 Woody Allen comedy Hannah and Her Sisters.

- Attorney Gary Bernstein is played by actor / comedian Jeff Altman who can also be seen in

Mork and Mindy, Maude, The Dukes of Hazzard, and the notoriously short-lived variety series Pink Lady and Jeff.
- Watch closely in part 2 of the story for an editing error. When Judge McGuire is talking with Grandma Harris, he is fiddling around with his pencil. When the scene cuts, the pencil is missing from his hands.

Barney the Gambler 2-1-81
The gang tries to help Barney when he gets in over his head with gambling debts.

Episode notes
- Archie refers to his problems with gambling in the season four-episode **Archie the Gambler**.
- The voice of the announcer is Ed Peck who previously appeared in the series in the season three-episode **Archie's Fraud** and the season five-episode **Archie's Contract**.

Murray Klein's Place 2-15-81
Murray walks out on Archie when he feels he is not getting an equal share in the business decisions.

Episode notes
- Arche references quitting the lodge (from the events earlier in the season in **The Incident**)

Weekend Away 2-22-81

Archie and Murray go to a restaurant vendor convention only to be held up in their hotel room.

Stephanie's Science Project 3-8-81

The gang helps Stephanie with her science project.

Episode notes

- Mark Lonow appears as Barry Bloom.
- This is the second and final appearance for Renne Jarrett as Mrs. Wakefield.

Tough Love 3-15-81

With Veronica's drinking out of control and affecting her work, Archie must stand firm that she stops or loses her job.

The Trashing of the Temple 3-29-81

Stephanie's temple is vandalized.

Episode notes

- Michael Mann reprises his role as Rabbi Jacobs. He can also be seen in the season six-episode **New Year's Wedding** (as the Reverend Harris), and **Gloria's False Alarm** (as Dr. Dolby) in season seven. He first appeared as Rabbi Jacobs in the season nine-episode **Stephanie's Conversion**.

La Cage Aux Bunker 4-5-81

Archie romances Stephanie's music teacher to get Stephanie a spot in the chorus.

Episode notes

- Carroll O'Connor wrote the story for this episode.
- Stephanie's teacher Victoria Springer is played by Olive Dunbar. Dunbar also appeared on such shows as Big John, Little John, Diff'rent Strokes, The Jeffersons, and Santa Barbara.
- When Archie leaves Miss Dunbar's room at the school, he gives a very W.C. Fieldsesque reaction when she starts to sing again.

Death of a Saint 5-3-81

Murray's Mother passes away while he is out with his new fiancé causing him to be consumed with guilt.

Goodbye, Murray 5-10-81

Murray moves to California with his fiancé.

season twelve episodes

Billie 10-4-81

Archie's niece Billie comes to live with him.

Episode notes

- Denise Miller is added to the cast as Billie. Her name will now appear in the opening credits.

- Billie is one of the four daughters of Archie's brother Fred. We have only met one of Fred's other daughters (Linda) in the season three-episode **Lionel Steps Out**.
- In the season nine episode **The Return of Archie's Brother**, his brother Fred is married to Catherine who is 18 years old. He is now married to Cindy who is 26.
- Archie tells Billie that she cooks like his mom.
- This episode marks a turning point in the series as slowly many of the story lines will shift to the younger cast with Archie becoming more of a supporting player.

The Business Manager 10-4-81
With Murray now gone, Archie's lawyer hires a business manager Roger Abbott to help straighten out the financial mess at the bar.

Episode notes
- This is the first of six series appearances for Gertrude Marx as the Rabinowitz's receptionist / secretary Lillian Fogelson.
- This is the first of two appearances for Steve Hendrickson as Roger Abbott.

The Date 10-11-81
Billie cozies up to Archie's new accountant to prove that Archie is too overprotective of her.

Episode notes
- Character actor Sydney Lassick can be seen in this episode as a customer appropriately named Syd. With over 80 screen appearances to his credit, he may be best known for his appearance as Cheswick in the 1976 film One Flew Over the Cuckoo's Nest.
- Steve Hendrickson makes his second and final appearance as Roger Abbott.

Norma Rae Bunker 10-18-81
Mrs. Canby takes a second job only she is unaware she is working for a sweatshop until she is swindled out of half of her pay.

Harry's Investment 10-25-81
Harry reveals that he is invested in McFeeny's Bar, a topless bar that is Archie's main competition.

Episode notes
- This is the second and final appearance for Sydney Lassick as Syd.
- Georgann Johnson makes her first of two appearances as Harry's wife Alice.
- This is Barry Gordon's first appearance as Gary Rabinowitz.
- Actress Jeannie Linero appears as a waitress at the topless bar. She previously appeared in the season one episode **Archie Gives Blood**, **Edith's**

Problem in season two, and the season seven episode **The Unemployment Story part II**.

Three's a Crowd 11-8-81
Barney meets a woman through computer dating but she only has eyes for Archie who struggles with his emotions since Edith's passing.

Episode notes
- This is the first of four appearances for Yvonne Wilder as Katherine Logan. Wilder began her screen career in the 1961 musical West Side Story and appeared in Room 222, The Partridge Family, Condo, and Gimme a Break!

Happy Birthday Stephanie 11-15-81
Billie gives Stephanie concert tickets for Devo for her birthday only Archie objects to the two of them going.

Episode notes
- The story of this episode is a slight reworking of the season two-episode Archie in the Lockup.
- If you wanted to see Devo at Madison Square Garden in 1981, it would set you back $15.

Growing Up is Hard to Do pt. 1 11-29-81
Growing Up is Hard to Do pt. 2 12-6-81
Stephanie celebrates her Bat Mitzvah as her father pays her a visit, causing problems between he and Archie.

Episode notes

- Celeste Holm returns as Estelle Harris.
- Mark Lonow appears as Barry Bloom.
- Ben Slack makes his second and final appearance as Stephanie's Father Floyd Mills. He was previously seen in the role in the season nine episode **The Return of Stephanie's Father**.
- Michael Mann makes his final series appearance as Rabbi Jacobs.
- The bit where the evangelists show up at the door and Archie closes it in their face is resurrected in this episode.

Stephanie's Dance 12-20-81

Archie has a hard time dealing with Stephanie attending her first school dance.

Episode notes

- Mark Lonow makes another appearance as Barry Bloom.

The Photo Contest 12-27-81

Archie's candid and not too flattering photos wind up being the hit of Stephanie's photo contest.

Episode notes

- Mark Lonow makes another appearance as Barry Bloom.

Stephanie's Tryout 1-3-82

Stephanie is the only girl to get a spot on her school's team.

The Night Visitor 1-17-82

Archie fears there is a thief sleeping in the storeroom, only to find out that Raoul has been staying there since being kicked out of his place.

Reggie-3; Archie-0 1-24-82

Archie gets himself in hot water when his truck gets into an accident with Reggie Jackson's car.

Episode notes

- Baseball legend Reggie Jackson appears in this episode.
- Barry Gordon makes another appearance as Gary Rabinowitz.

Blind Man's Bluff 1-31-82

Mr. Van Ranseleer is mugged on his way home, causing him to withdraw and stay in his apartment.

Episode notes

- The theme of this episode is somewhat reminiscent of **Gloria, the Victim** from season three and **Edith's Fiftieth Birthday** from season eight.
- This is the first appearance of William Boyett as Lt. Jim Carmody. He will begin dating Veronica.

A Blast from the Past 2-7-82

An old flame from Billie's past resurfaces in hopes of getting back together with her.

Episode notes

- Barry Gordon appears again as Gary Rabinowitz.
- Billie and Gary begin seeing one another in this episode.
- The part of Ted Green is played by series producer Alan Rosen.
- Take notice that Ted Green has an American Flag on his jacket lapel much the same as Archie has on his lumberjack coat.

Sex and the Single Parent 2-21-82

Archie opposes to Stephanie taking a sex education class until he overhears that one of her friends is pregnant.

Episode notes

- The part of Ronald Scott is played by versatile character actor Alan Fudge who appeared on many television shows including Eishied, Lou Grant, Little House on the Prairie, 7th Heaven, How I Met Your Mother, Big Love, and The Closer. He may be best known to M*A*S*H fans as Captain Arnold Chandler, who thinks he is Jesus Christ in the classic episode "Quo Vadis, Captain Chandler?". His last television

role was in an episode of The Office in 2009. Fudge passed away on October 10, 2011
- Mark Lonow makes his final appearance as Barry Bloom.

Gloria Comes Home (part I and part II) 2-28-82
Gloria returns home to start a fresh life after leaving Michael and is used as a springboard for the spinoff series Gloria.

Episode notes
- While originally aired in a one-hour timeslot, this is split into two episodes and airs as such in syndication.
- This episode marks the final appearance of Barbara Meek as Mrs. Canby. There is no explanation ever given for her departure. Meek went on to do work in PBS movies and soap operas such as As the World Turns and The Guiding Light. Meek passed away on October 3, 2015
- This episode is co-directed (with Gary Shimokawa) by Carroll O'Connor.
- Screen legend Burgess Meredith makes an appearance as Dr. Willard Adams and will go on to co-star in the spinoff Gloria. Meredith is best known to television viewers on the hit 1960s series Batman as well as Mickey in the first three films of the Rocky franchise.

- Christopher Johnson plays Joey Stivic. He will be replaced by Christian Jacobs when Gloria premieres the following Fall.

Of Mice and Bunker 3-7-82

A con-artist tries to take over Archie's Place when Archie is forced to find a buyer for Murray's share.

Episode notes

- Actor Joe Mantegna plays Joe Garver. Up to this point, Mantegna did series work in shows like Soap, Bosom Buddies, and It's a Living. He would soon branch out into feature film work co-starring in The Godfather: Part III (1990) and Searching for Bobby Fischer (1993). On television he has portrayed David Rossi since 2005 on Criminal Minds and its current incarnation Criminal Minds: Evolution.
- The part of Larry Billings is played by Ian Patrick Williams who also did spots on Hill Street Blues, Married With Children, ER, Dexter, and Ray Donovan.

Relapse 3-14-82

When her ex-husband Carmine returns to town, Veronica has a relapse with alcohol.

Episode notes

- Jerry Stiller makes his second and final appearance as Carmine.

- This is Anne Meara's final appearance in the series and no explanation will be given as to what happened to her.
- William Boyett returns as Veronica's boyfriend Jim Carmody.

Love is Hell 3-21-82

A boy that Stephanie is interested in puts the moves on Billie.

The Second Time Around 3-28-82

Katherine returns and the romantic interest between her and Archie is rekindled.

Episode notes

- Yvonne Wilder returns as Katherine Logan.

West Side Astoria 4-4-82

Katherine introduces Archie to her uptight family and things do not go very well for him.

Episode notes

- Archie and Katherine are dating for six months in this episode.
- Luis Avalos appears as John Hernandez. With over 600 credits to his name, he was part of the ensemble cast of The Electric Company. He also appeared in Soap, was a co-star in the one season MacLean Stevenson sitcom Condo, and NYPD Blue.

- Carmen Zapata stars as Mrs. Hernandez. She can also be seen in episodes of Kojak, The Streets of San Francisco, Harry O, Trapper John, M.D., and made almost 60 appearances in the daytime soap Santa Barbara.

Billie Moves Out 4-11-82

Feeling closed in by an overbearing Archie, Billie moves out…and in with Gary.

Episode notes

- Barry Gordon appears as Gary Rabinowitz.

Rabinowitz's Brother 5-2-82

Gary and his brother Barry are at odds over Gary's abilities, igniting a lifelong rivalry.

Episode notes

- Barry Gordon appears as Gary Rabinowitz.
- Allan Miller makes the first of four appearances as Barry Rabinowitz. Miller has also appeared on Knots Landing, Quincy M.E., Soap, Dallas, Murder, She Wrote, and Mad Men.
- Gertrude Marx makes her second appearance as Lillian Fogelson.
- In the scene where Billie tells Archie she will be sorry for firing Gary, Archie says he will get his older brother "Gary" to help instead of calling him "Barry".

Death of a Lodger 5-9-82

In need of extra money, Barney takes in a boarder.

Episode notes

- Stand-up and legend Don Rickles portrays Al Snyder. Rickles is well known for his insult style of comedy and was once labeled "the merchant of venom". Rickles made appearances in numerous television shows including The Munsters, Get Smart, The Beverly Hillbillies, The Andy Griffith Show, and The Larry Sanders Show. He is also known for several failed attempts at sitcoms to feature him including The Don Rickles Show, CPO Sharkey, and Daddy Dearest. He succeeded best on television in the variety / talk show format including The Dean Martin Show, The Dean Martin Celebrity Roasts, and numerous appearances on both The Tonight Show starring Johnny Carson and The Late Show starring David Letterman. His feature film work includes Kelly's Heroes (1970), Casino (1995), and the voice of Mr. Potato Head in the Toy Story franchise. Rickles died April 6, 2017
- Johnny Brown appears as Mr. Johnson who is interested in renting the room from Barney. Brown is best known as Bookman from the Norman Lear series Good Times. He was also one of the featured players on Rowan and Martin's Laugh-In.

- If you look closely at the scene after Al dies, the shots do not match. His hand moves from the arm of the chair in one shot to his stomach in the next.
- Archie reminds Barney that he once took in a boarder (a reference to Teresa Betancourt).
- This episode is co-directed (with Gary Shimokawa) by Carroll O'Connor.

The Battle of Bunker III 5-16-82

Stephanie becomes jealous of all the attention Archie is paying to Catherine.

Episode notes

- This is the final series appearance for Yvonne Wilder as Catherine Logan.
- The movie they want to go see in this episode is Annie. Danielle Brisebois was in the original Broadway cast of Annie prior to joining the cast of All in the Family.

season thirteen episodes

Archie's Night Out 9-26-82

Archie, Harry, and Barney go out looking for dates.

Episode notes

- Barry Gordon, Abraham Alvarez, and Joe Rosario are all added to the cast in the opening credits.

- Archie mentions at the beginning of the episode that he and Catherine have broken up.
- The part of Joanie is played by Joan Shawlee who can also be seen in such feature films as the Abbott and Costello comedy Buck Privates Come Home (1947), Some Like It Hot (1959), and The Apartment (1960).

Gary's Ex 10-3-82

Gary's ex-girlfriend returns to town causing conflict between he and Billie.

The Eyewitnesses 10-10-82

Jose and Raoul are witnesses to a robbery and are hesitant to say anything because of their immigration status.

Episode notes
- William Boyett makes his final appearance as Lt. Jim Carmody.
- Gertrude Marx makes another appearance as Lillian Fogelson.

Double Date 10-17-82

Gary and Billie double date with Stephanie so she can impress a boy she likes.

Episode notes

- Danny Ferguson is played by Brian Robbins who turned to producing such shows as Smallville, One Tree Hill. Freakish, and Zac and Mia.

From the Waldorf to Astoria 10-24-82

Archie's Place holds an art auction when it is discovered that Jose exhibits some artistic talent.

Episode notes

- Richard Stahl (Mr. Sanborn) is an All in the Family alum who also appeared in the season one-episode **Archie's Aching Back** and the season four-episode **Archie Eats and Runs**.

Stay Out of My Briefs 10-31-82

Billie takes on a second job as Gary's secretary

Episode notes

- Allan Miller makes his second appearance as Barry Rabinowitz.
- Gertrude Marx appears again as Lillian Fogelson.

Break a Leg, Stephanie 11-7-82

Stephanie auditions for an elite music school.

Episode notes

- Mark Price plays one of the audition hopefuls and is probably best known to Family Ties fans as Skippy.

Archie Gets a Head 11-21-82

Archie installs a second bathroom in the basement.

Barney Gets Laid Off 11-28-82

Barney feels depressed after losing his job.

Marriage On the Rocks 12-12-82

When Archie stands up a date, Harry steps in and begins an extramarital affair.

Episode notes

- Georgann Johnson makes her second and final appearance as Alice Snowden.

Father Christmas 12-19-82

Archie's Brother Fred returns for a Christmas visit which causes some pain for Billie.

Episode notes

- The bit where Archie slams the door in the face of an evangelist is again revived again in this episode.
- When Fred first arrives at the house, he gently touches Edith's chair in a sweet acknowledgement of the deceased character.

Teacher's Pet 12-26-82

Impressed by a teacher, Billie helps him out by doing some extra work until he makes a pass at her.

Captain Video 1-2-83

Barney joins a shady video dating service.

The Promotion 1-9-83

Gary is at odds again with his brother for a promotion at the family firm.

Episode notes

- Allan Miller makes another appearance as Barry Rabinowitz.

Three Women 1-16-83

Stephanie spends the weekend with her grandmother and becomes angry when she will not discuss her mother with her.

Episode notes

- Celeste Holm makes her final appearance as Estelle Harris.
- Character actress Mitzi Hoag appears as Cousin Sophie. Hoag appeared on My Three Sons, The Partridge Family, Mod Squad, and Here Come the Brides in addition to over 70 other credits.

Relief Bartender 1-23-83

To ease the workload, Archie's Place hires a relief bartender yet Archie hesitates when the best candidate is a woman causing her to sue for discrimination.

Episode notes

- Fern Fitzgerald makes her first appearance as Pat McBride. She will appear three more times. Her addition this late in the series is a curious one. After this initial interaction, her and Archie do not have any tension between them for which to further develop her character.

The Red Herring 1-30-83

While throwing a birthday party for Mr. Van Ranseleer, Archie realizes he was accused of being a Communist in the 1950s.

Episode notes

- Brendan Dillon plays a customer of Archie's Place. Perhaps he would be more comfortable behind the bar as he previously appeared as Kelsey in the season two episodes **Mike's Problem** and **Archie is Jealous**, and the season three episodes **Archie and the Editorial** and **Gloria and the Riddle**.

The Boys' Night Out 2-13-83

Archie, Harry, and Barney go out for a night on the town to celebrate their friendship and mistakenly wind up in a gay bar.

Episode notes

- Fern Fitzgerald appears again as Pat McBride.
- Brendan Dillon makes another appearance as a customer.

I Can Manage 2-20-83

Archie falls for a woman who is speaking at a restaurant seminar and spends the night with her, unaware that she is married.

Store Wars 2-27-83

Murray returns to Archie's Place to unload his share of the bar.

Episode notes

- Martin Balsam guest stars as Murray Klein.
- Murray mentions he is also in town to see his daughter and grandson only in her first visit (in season ten's **Murray's Daughter**) she tells him he has two grandkids.
- This is the only episode that mentions Veronica is no longer working at Archie's Place.
- Murray refers to the time Archie almost shot him in the season ten episode **The Ambush**.
- The price for Murray's share of the business is $40,000.
- This episode marks the final appearance of Gertrude Marx as Lillian Fogelson.
- Allan Miller makes his final appearance as Barry Rabinowitz.
- This episode is co-directed (along with Gary Shimokawa) by Carroll O'Connor.

Bunker Madness 3-13-83

Billie covers for Stephanie when Archie finds marijuana in the house.

No One Said it Was Easy 3-27-83

Gary and Billie decide they no longer want to see one another.

Episode notes

- Fern Fitzgerald makes her third appearance as Pat McBride.

Small Claims Court 3-28-83

In support of Barney's new job at an electronics store, Archie buys a TV and winds up in court.

Episode notes

- Prolific character actor Parley Baer appears as Judge Anthony Barzini. Baer had nearly 300 credits on his resume including appearances on Make Room for Daddy, The Andy Griffith Show, The Adventures of Ozzie and Harriet, The Adams Family, Perry Mason, Hogan's Heroes, The Dukes of Hazard, and The Golden Girls.

I'm Torn Here 4-4-83

After she goes on a date with another man, Billie and Gary discuss how to move on as friends after their break-up.

Episode notes

- Fern Fitzgerald makes her final appearance as Pat McBride.

Afterword

For any other actor with an iconic role like Archie Bunker on his resume, one would think work would be impossible to find for Carroll O'Connor. However, in the wake of the cancellation of Archie Bunker's Place, O'Connor successfully returned to the stage and struck gold again on television as Bill Gillespie in the series In the Heat of the Night. Based on the 1967 feature film starring Sidney Poitier and Rod Steiger, the series ran for eight years and O'Connor picked up another Emmy. After that show ended, he had a recurring role on Party of Five as well as playing Helen Hunt's father in several episodes of Mad About You. O'Connor made headlines after his adopted son Hugh committed suicide in 1995. O'Connor publicly went after the drug dealer who in turn sued him for slander. The jury found in favor of O'Connor. Hugh had been a drug addict for several years and because of his death, Carroll O'Connor spearheaded the passing the Drug Dealer Civil Liability Act which is on the books in some states. The law allows families of the deceased to sue for compensation in civil court. O'Connor told Dateline in 1997 "My son's dead. There isn't a day I don't miss him and want him back in the worst way. I want him back today, now. I won't get him back....it's not over until I die."[63] O'Connor's final role was that of Minnie Driver's father in the 2000 comedy Return to Me. He died of a heart attack on June 21, 2001.

Jean Stapleton related in a 2000 interview with the Archive of American Television. "I only saw it once while we were making the series. I'd look at it critically and that was it and I never watched the show thereafter. But now that all this time has elapsed I can watch totally objectively and I love it. And I laugh and think "Gee, that's good."[64] Moving away from the role of such an iconic character required careful selection of material for the talented actor. "Truck drivers would call at me if they spot me on the street and yell out "Edith!"" In other circles, I made sure to turn down any parts that would suggest the character of Edith Bunker because I didn't want to be buried and typecast in that kind of part....it would limit my opportunities for employment."[65] Stapleton was offered the role ultimately taken by Angela Lansbury in the CBS drama Murder, She Wrote but she turned it down. Her first love was the theatre and that is where she returned. Among many other performances, she portrayed Julia Child in "Bon Appetit" as well as Eleanor Roosevelt in a one-woman show (a role she originally portrayed in a TV film for CBS in 1982). She also alternated between film and television work guesting on such series as Caroline in the City, Murphy Brown, Everybody Loves Raymond, and Touched by an Angel. Her most notable feature film work was in Michael (1996) and the 1998 rom-com You've Got Mail. She was reunited with Carroll O'Connor one final time on April 24th, 2000 when they appeared together on The Donny and Marie talk show. She died of natural causes on May 31, 2013.

Rob Reiner still acts (appearing in such films as The First Wives Club (1996) and The Wolf of Wall Street (2013)) and is known as one of the most successful directors in the past 40 plus years with feature film credits such as This Is Spinal Tap (1984), Stand by Me (1986), The Princess Bride (1987), When Harry Met Sally (1989), Misery (1990), and A Few Good Men (1992), Reiner has created an iconic body of work and continues to be involved in social activism. Among his involvement in many other organizations, he is the co-founder of the American Foundation for Equal Rights. The foundation was instrumental in overturning Proposition 8 in California (a law which banned same-sex marriage).

After the cancellation of Gloria, Sally Struthers went back to the stage in a female version of The Odd Couple and became an advocate and spokesperson for the Save the Children charity. The talented actress continued stage work in such productions as Grease, The Best Little Whorehouse in Texas, Cat on a Hot Tin Roof, and Steel Magnolias. Struthers also returned to episodic television in 1986 when she replaced Rita Moreno in the syndicated version of 9 to 5. She carved out a niche doing voice work in several animated series and is probably best known to modern audiences as Babette Dell in the series Gilmore Girls and its Netflix reboot Gilmore Girls: A Year in the Life where she co-stars with All in the Family alum Liz Torres.

Norman Lear continued to stay busy with television projects and social activism. He published his memoir "Even This I Get to Experience" in 2014. Most recently he Executive Produced the reboot of One Day at a Time for the Netflix streaming service. The show had a respectable 4 season run before its cancellation in 2020. Lear passed away on December 5, 2023 at 101 years old.

All in the Family was clearly a case of being in the right place at the right time. The counterculture and civil rights movements that defined the 1960s gave way to more open and honest expression as America ushered in the 1970s. There was a divide between the generations and All in the Family was the first show on television that reflected the times and did so using comedy and satire as a base for its theatre. Each character reacted out of love and fear and found that many times they were both sides of the same coin. It neither glorified or exploited either side of an issue. It was immediate, current, and presented real-life situations in a humorous tone that were relatable. Through its art, All in the Family paved the way for more freedom of expression on television. Its influence on the medium was instantaneous with copycat shows springing up almost overnight and its impact and influence has extended past the decade in which the show was originally produced. It set a trend that television can be topical and yet still entertain in both comedic and dramatic fashion. In 1994, Norman Lear himself tried to update the premise when 704 Hauser premiered on the CBS network. Starring John Amos as liberal patriarch Ernie Cumberbatch (perhaps a nod to the surname Archie referred to several times in the series), the lead character had purchased Archie's old house and had a conservative son and a Jewish daughter in law. Although six episodes were produced, the series only lasted five weeks and was cancelled. With all due respect to the vision of its creator to adapt the material, All in the Family was that special. It captured the pulse of the country which was at war with itself on almost every level during its most tumultuous period. While on Jay Leno in 1997, promoting his role in the upcoming film Return to Me, Carroll O'Connor told the host that he had an idea to resurrect his beloved character. Archie sold the bar, moved to Manhattan, and went into a "car hire service" with some of his old buddies. When Leno enthusiastically responded that it sounded like a great idea, O'Connor said that Norman Lear would not let him have the rights to the character.

Over 50 years after All in the Family premiered, the way people watch television has changed dramatically. Network television seems to be defined by a sea of reality-based shows that are cheaply produced and exploitive by nature. Yet, with more viewing choices these days between cable and streaming, there is still challenging and compelling programming of quality being produced. A show like Veep is well written and cleverly captures the satirical side of politics whereas reboots such as Roseanne and Murphy Brown are more calculated in their approach to the current social and political climate. When All in the Family premiered, although criticized at times, it had no such agenda. It set out to tell stories we could all relate to through characters we all knew in our everyday lives. That was the genius of the show. While some of the references may be dated which is inherent in many older shows, the themes are still very relevant. No matter what decade we may currently occupy, there is always a time in our lives we look back on and say "those were the days." The crew and actors left behind a body of work that will live on and continue to be discovered and discussed. In a time of reboot happy networks, a series like this seems ripe for revisiting yet it is unlikely it would ever sustain.

On May 22, 2019, ABC aired "Live in Front of a Studio Audience and adapted the script from the season four-episode **Henry's Farewell** (along with a script of The Jeffersons). While everyone looks like they are enjoying themselves, the production was woefully miscast and poorly executed with Woody Harrelson as Archie and Marisa Tomei as Edith. Hosted by Jimmy Kimmel and Norman Lear, the actors performed the script as the title suggests – in front of a live audience. The audience was generous in its response to the mostly uninspired presentation of the material which had the feel of a neighborhood theater production. The show however did attract over 10 million viewers and had a strong enough showing for ABC to do it again. On December 18, the script for **The Draft Dodger** (along with a script from Good Times) was performed with Harrelson and Tomei reprising their roles. While it did not attract nearly as many viewers (who more than likely tuned in to the first episode for curiosity's sake) ABC had enough faith in the concept for a third go around and in December of 2021 aired another installment but this time featured scripts from The Facts of Life and Diff'rent Strokes. The performance of Henry's Farewell won an Emmy for Outstanding Live Variety Special and while acknowledged by the Academy, these shows are unnecessary and say more about the state of development in network television today than anything else. Perhaps a better presentation would have been to show the original episodes to an audience mixed of different generations and then follow up with a Q&A to discuss reactions to the material seen through the eyes of today's viewers. Or, perhaps it is better to leave it all alone.

All in the Family was a unique program and came at the perfect time when the country could accept such topics being discussed in a satirical manner while maintaining respect for different points of view. It has made a lasting mark in the history of television. Those were the days indeed.

References

1   E! True Hollywood Story: All in the Family – E! Network 2000

2   E! True Hollywood Story: All in the Family – E! Network 2000

3   E! True Hollywood Story: All in the Family – E! Network 2000

4   E! True Hollywood Story: All in the Family – E! Network 2000

5   "Those Were the Days: The Birth Of "All in the Family" – documentary Shout Factory 2012

6   "Those Were the Days: The Birth Of "All in the Family" – documentary Shout Factory 2012

7   "The Boy Next Door to the Bunkers" – Dwight Whitney TV Guide June 2, 1973

8   Television Academy Foundation: The Interviews; Remembering Former CBS Standards and Practices Executive William Tankersley 2/22/16

9   "The Television Revolution Begins: All in the Family is on the Air" – documentary Shout Factory 2012

10 "The Television Revolution Begins: All in the Family is on the Air" – documentary Shout Factory 2012

11 "The Television Revolution Begins: All in the Family is on the Air" – documentary Shout Factory 2012

12 "The Television Revolution Begins: All in the Family is on the Air" – documentary Shout Factory 2012

13 Hollywood Reporter Review. Sue Cameron January 12, 1971

14 Hollywood Reporter Review. Sue Cameron January 12, 1971

15 E! True Hollywood Story: All in the Family – E! Network 2000

16 "Stormy Years With Archie" – Carroll O'Connor TV Guide September 22, 1979

17 "For the Dingbat, These Are the Days" – Dwight Whitney TV Guide 5-27-72

18 Carroll O'Connor on the Dick Cavett Show December 8, 1971

19 "Those Were the Days: The Birth Of "All in the Family" – documentary Shout Factory 2012

20 Television Academy Foundation; The Interviews; Jean Stapleton November 28, 2000

21 New interview with Norman Lear – Shout Factory 2012

22 Television Academy Foundation; The Interviews; Jean Stapleton November 28, 2000

23 Television Academy Foundation; The Interviews; Jean Stapleton November 28, 2000

24 Television Academy Foundation; The Interviews; Jean Stapleton November 28, 2000

25 "The Television Revolution Begins: All in the Family is on the Air" – documentary Shout Factory 2012

26 "The Television Revolution Begins: All in the Family is on the Air" – documentary Shout Factory 2012

27 "Stormy Years With Archie" – Carroll O'Connor TV Guide September 22, 1979

28 "The Television Revolution Begins: All in the Family is on the Air" – documentary Shout Factory 2012

29 "Stormy Years With Archie" – Carroll O'Connor TV Guide September 22, 1979

30 E! True Hollywood Story: All in the Family – E! Network 2000

31 Television Academy Foundation; The Interviews; Rob Reiner November 29, 2004

32 "The Television Revolution Begins: All in the Family is on the Air" – documentary Shout Factory 2012

33 "The Television Revolution Begins: All in the Family is on the Air" – documentary Shout Factory 2012

34 "The Television Revolution Begins: All in the Family is on the Air" – documentary Shout Factory 2012

35 "The Television Revolution Begins: All in the Family is on the Air" – documentary Shout Factory 2012

36 Television Academy Foundation; The Interviews; Betty Garrett May 21, 2003

37 "Those Were the Days: The Birth Of "All in the Family" – documentary Shout Factory 2012

38 Television Academy Foundation; The Interviews; Jean Stapleton November 28, 2000

39 E! True Hollywood Story: All in the Family – E! Network 2000

40 Associated Press interview (MeTV article September 19, 2023)

41 E! True Hollywood Story: All in the Family – E! Network 2000

42 "Stormy Years With Archie" – Carroll O'Connor TV Guide September 22, 1979

43 "The Television Revolution Begins: All in the Family is on the Air" – documentary Shout Factory 2012

44 "Sally Struthers Says 'All in the Family' Cast Got Along 'Beautifully': 'There Wasn't Competition'" – Katie Bruno / Closer Staff August 1, 2021

45 "Farewell to the Family" – People Magazine March 28, 1978

46 "Farewell to the Family" – People Magazine March 28, 1978

47 E! True Hollywood Story: All in the Family – E! Network 2000

48 "Farewell to the Family" – People Magazine March 28, 1978

49 "Farewell to the Family" – People Magazine March 28, 1978

50 "Farewell to the Family" – People Magazine March 28, 1978

51 "Stormy Years With Archie" – Carroll O'Connor TV Guide September 22, 1979

52 "Stormy Years With Archie" – Carroll O'Connor TV Guide September 22, 1979

53 Television Academy Foundation; The Interviews; Jean Stapleton November 28, 2000

54 "Why Archie Survives" – Dwight Whitney TV Guide August 8, 1981

55 "Why Archie Survives" – Dwight Whitney TV Guide August 8, 1981

56 "Why Archie Survives" – Dwight Whitney TV Guide August 8, 1981

57 "Why Archie Survives" – Dwight Whitney TV Guide August 8, 1981

58 "Sex On TV: How to Protect Your Children" – Dorothy Singer and Jerome Singer August 7, 1982

59 "Archie Bunker, Stifled; CBS Drops O'Connor Show From Fall Lineup" – Tom Shales May 11, 1983

60 "Archie Bunker, Stifled; CBS Drops O'Connor Show From Fall Lineup" –
Tom Shales May 11, 1983

61 "Archie Bunker, Stifled; CBS Drops O'Connor Show From Fall Lineup" –
Tom Shales May 11, 1983

62 "Archie Bunker, Stifled; CBS Drops O'Connor Show From Fall Lineup" –
Tom Shales May 11, 1983

63 Dateline: Carroll O'Connor 1997

64 Television Academy Foundation; The Interviews; Jean Stapleton
November 28, 2000

65 Television Academy Foundation; The Interviews; Jean Stapleton
November 28, 2000

Printed in the United States
by Baker & Taylor Publisher Services